ᚠᚢᚦᚨᚱᚲᚷᚹᚺᚾᛁᛃᛇᛈᛉᛊᛏᛒᛖᛗᛚᛜᛟᛞ

Northern Lore

A Field Guide to

The Northern Mind-Body-Sprit

Eoghan Odinsson

ᚠᚢᚦᚨᚱᚲᚷᚹᚺᚾᛁᛃᛇᛈᛉᛊᛏᛒᛖᛗᛚᛜᛟᛞ

Visit my website at www.eoghanodinsson.com

Printed in the United States of America

First Printing: June 2010

Second Edition: February 2012

ISBN 1452851433

EAN-13 9781452851433

Typeset in Garamond 12pt

By the same Author:

Northern Wisdom

The Runes in 9 minutes

Northern Plant Lore

A Door in the Woods - Coming Summer 2012

Dedication:

I humbly dedicate this work to J.R.R. Tolkien who has inspired and shaped the lives of countless people with his immortal work.

His use of our own folkore and history as a foundation for his epic works of fiction, sparked a renaissance and passion for the soul of our people – our Folklore.

Cattle die and kinsmen die,
thyself too must die,
but one thing never dies, --
fame of one who has earned it.
- Havamal

Acknowledgements

I would like to thank the following people who have made this book not only possible, but joyful..

My wife, for being my sanctuary.

My son, who has made me a better man in every way.

Dave Heard, my good friend and neighbour who encouraged my serious study of the Runes - glad I "Heard" the call.

Jimmy Wales and Larry Sanger – co-founders of Wikipedia. I believe Wikipedia may prove to be the greatest educational resource for the 21'st Century.

There are several websites that I visit regularly and would like to give them special mention here:

www.gutenberg.org – Project Gutenberg is the first and largest single collection of free electronic books, or eBooks. Michael Hart, founder of Project Gutenberg, invented eBooks in 1971 and continues to inspire the creation of eBooks and related technologies today.

www.eddan.net - Mats Wendt is a visionary composer and conducter who invented the concept of the Cybersymphony. He has created a 16+ hour cybersymphony around the entire set of Eddas. An amazing modern legacy, and accessible on his website at no cost.

About the Author

Canadian born Eoghan Odinsson is an award winning journalist and author with a lifelong passion for the knowledge of our Northern forefathers – or "folk lore". Literally, the knowledge of our people.

Graduating from the University of Aberdeen in Scotland with his Masters of Science degree, he subsequently taught for the University, and was a dissertation advisor for graduate students.

In addition to his academic background, Eoghan also holds a Black Belt in Shito-Ryu Karate, and has taught Martial Arts in Canada and the USA.

Eoghan currently lives in the Washington D.C. area with his wife, son and three dogs.

Contents

Foreword

So what is this book? Why am I sharing this with you? I'm glad you asked!

I've spent a good deal of my life researching and reflecting on the knowledge of our ancestors. Inspired initially by the works of authors like Tolkien and C.S. Lewis, I began to dig into the real history behind the fabulous tales I read; the library became my second home. The Lord of the Rings for example, has its roots in Teutonic mythology. The Runes Tolkien presented in the first edition of The Hobbit were in fact Anglo-Saxon runes that were in daily use 1500+ years ago as a system of writing and tribal magic.

As the years passed, I was exposed to more knowledge than I could ever imagine existed (thanks to the advent of the Internet), and connected with people across the globe with similar interests. I suddenly found myself learning about herb lore, martial arts, navigation, and other knowledge with ties to our Northern ancestors. What a legacy!

There are excellent books on the history of our ancestors, some on the physical crafts of our folk, and many on the spiritual or esoteric aspects of those traditions – runic divination, galdr (chanting) etc. However, to my knowledge, none have presented a view touching on all those aspects - presenting a sampling of lore from the whole of our ancestral corpus – the mind-body-spirit. Clearly I can't cover everything in one volume, so what I will do, is introduce you to some very interesting examples, and follow up with additional books devoted to an in depth treatment of many of the topics.

This book will highlight the lore as we understand it, based on archaeological evidence, extant written sources, and present day manifestations of that lore.

Together I hope we can take an incredible journey back in time, and forward, embracing a synthesis of ancestral riches, and modern sensibilities. My hope is that after reading this, you'll go and dig deeper into your history – read the Eddas, harvest some herbs, practice runic yoga and cook a Viking feast!

Live the Lore!

Eoghan Odinsson, June, 2010

Conventions

1. **A note on modern conventions used:**
   - BCE=Before Common Era (aka. BC)
   - CE=Common Era (aka. AD)
2. **Pronounciation:**
   - Eth (Ð, ð; also spelled edh or eð) is a letter used in Old English, Icelandic, Faroese (in which it is called edd), and Elfdalian. It was also used in Scandinavia during the Middle Ages, but was subsequently replaced with dh and later d. The capital eth resembles a D with a line partially through the vertical stroke. The lower case resembles an insular d with a line through the top - **ð represents a sound like th in English "them".**

   - Thorn, or þorn (Þ, þ), is a letter in the Old English and Icelandic alphabets, as well as some dialects of Middle English. It was also used in medieval Scandinavia, but was later replaced with the digraph th. The letter originated from the rune Þ in the Elder Fuþark, called thorn in the Anglo-Saxon and thorn or thurs ("giant") in the Scandinavian rune poems, its reconstructed Proto-Germanic name being *Thurisaz. - **Þ represents a sound like th in English "thick".**

   - J in many of the Scandinavaian dialects was pronoucned like a **Y**, or **long I**, so you will see words with either a J or I which for the most part represents the same "Yuh' sound.

Page Intentionally Blank

ᛈᚿᚦᚠᚱᚲᚷᛈᚺᛁᛈᛇᛃᚴᚠᛋᛏᛒᛗᛘᛚᛜᛟ

Part 1
Mind of the North

ᛈᚿᚦᚠᚱᚲᚷᛈᚺᛁᛈᛇᛃᚴᚠᛋᛏᛒᛗᛘᛚᛜᛟ

> **Folk:** Of or pertaining to the inhabitants of a land, their culture, tradition, or history.
>
> **Lore:** All the facts and traditions about a particular subject that have been accumulated over time through education or experience.

In Part 1, we'll review some of the history and **exoteric**[1] knowledge of our ancestors.

We'll start by taking a look at some of the notable tribes and civilizations that have contributed to our lore, move onto an overview of the runes, and finish up with a look at some weather lore.

---

[1] Exoteric refers to knowledge that is outside of and independent from anyone's experience and can be ascertained by anyone. In effect it is "Common Sense". It is distinguished from esoteric knowledge. Exoteric relates to "external reality" as opposed to one's own thoughts or feelings. It is knowledge that is public as opposed to secretive or cabalistic. It is not required that exoteric knowledge come easily or automatically, but it should be referenceable or reproducible.

If you would understand anything, observe its beginning and its development.
- Aristotle

Chapter 1 – Legacy of the Northmen

rom the cold and frozen fjords of Scandinavia, to heavily forested Germania, and west to the fertile, temperate British Isles, came the men and women of the North. Forged into hardy and resourceful tribes by necessity; they wandered far in search of riches, fame, and new places to call home. It is from this most noble and courageous stock, many of us claim descent.

Just Another Day?

One of the most overlooked legacies of our Northern Ancestors is codified in the Days of the Week in the English Language; all but Saturday, are named for one of our old Germanic gods and goddesses.

When I first discovered this, I was perplexed that such an obvious piece of our culture was never taught in school to my generation, or that of my children. We learn about Roman and Greek Mythology in most North American schools (which I thoroughly enjoyed as a child), but not about Germanic/Norse mythology, when approximately 65% of the population of America is of North Western European descent.

In the Preface of his 1897 version of the "Younger Edda", Rasmus B. Anderson, LL. D. has the following to say:

"The records of our Teutonic past have hitherto received but slight attention from the English-speaking branch of the great world-ash Yggdrasil. This indifference is the more deplorable, since a knowledge of our heroic forefathers would naturally operate as a most powerful means of keeping alive among us, and our posterity, that spirit of courage, enterprise and independence for which the old Teutons were so distinguished."

Lets walk through some of the fascinating lore behind our "everyday" lives.

Sunday

In Old English Sunday was Sunnandæg (pronounced [sun.nan.dæg], meaning "Sun's Day". This is a translation of the Latin phrase Dies Solis. English, like most of the Germanic languages, preserves the original pagan/sun associations of the day. Many other European languages, including all of the Romance languages, have changed its name to the equivalent of "the Lord's day" (based on Ecclesiastical Latin Dies Dominica). In both West Germanic and North Germanic mythology the sun is personified as a goddess; Sunna/Sól.

Monday

Old English Mōnandæg (pronounced [mon.nan.dæg], meaning "Moon's Day". This is likely based on a translation of the Latin name Dies Lunae. In North Germanic mythology, the moon is personified as a god; **Mani.**

4

Figure 1 - "The Wolves Pursuing Sol and Mani" (1909) by J. C. Dollman

Tuesday

Old English Tiwesdæg (pronounced [ti.wes.dæg], meaning "Tiw's day." Tiw (Norse **Tyr**) was a god associated with law, justice and pledges in Norse mythology and also attested prominently in wider Germanic paganism.; Tyr is also known for being one-handed, after he lost his hand to the Fenris wolf in order to save his people. The name of the day is based on Latin Dies Martis, "Day of Mars" (the Roman war god).

Wednesday

Old English Wōdnesdæg (pronounced [wo:d.nes.dæg], meaning the day of the Germanic god Wodan (later known as **Odin** among the North Germanic peoples), and a prominent god of the Anglo-Saxons (and other Germanic peoples) in England until about the seventh century. It is likely based on the Latin Dies Mercurii, "Day of Mercury". The usual explanation is that both Wodan and Mercury were considered psychopomps, or leaders of souls, in their respective mythologies; both are also associated with poetic and musical inspiration. German Mittwoch and Finnish keskiviikko both mean 'mid-week'.

Thursday: Old English Thūnresdæg (pronounced [Thu:n.res.dæg], meaning the Thunor's day. Thunor is commonly known in Modern English as **Thor**, the god of thunder in Germanic Heathenism. It is based on the Latin Dies Iovis, "Day of Jupiter". In the Roman pantheon, Jupiter was the chief god, who seized and maintained his power on the basis of his thunderbolt.

Friday

Old English Frigedæg (pronounced [fri.je.dæg], meaning the day of the Anglo-Saxon goddess Fríge, and is attested among the North Germanic peoples as **Frigg**. It is based on the Latin Dies Veneris, "Day of Venus". Venus was the Roman goddess of beauty, love and sex.

Saturday

The only day of the week to retain its Roman origin in English, named after the Roman god Saturn associated with the Titan Cronus, father of Zeus and many Olympians. Its original Anglo-Saxon rendering was Sæturnesdæg (pronounced [sæ.tur.nes.dæg]. In Latin it was Dies Saturni, "Day of Saturn". The Spanish and Portuguese Sábado, the Romanian Sâmbătă, and the Italian Sabato come from Sabbata Dies (Day of the Sabbath).

      The Germanic peoples adapted the system for the days of the week introduced by the Romans, but replaced the Roman deities (with the exception of Saturday) with their indigenous gods - in a process known as **Interpretatio germanica.** According to Rudolf Simek, this occurred around the 1st century CE when both cultures came into closer contact, and the only reliable insight into interpretatio germanica can be found in the Germanic translations of the Roman names for the days of the week:

- The day of Mars is translated as the day of Ziu/Tyr (Tuesday).
- The day of Mercury is translated as the day of Wodan/Odin (Wednesday).
- The day of Jupiter is translated as the day of Donar/Thor, though Thor is generally identified in interpretatio romana as Hercules. (Thursday)
- The day of Venus is translated as the day of Frija/Frigg. (Friday)

Day	Germanic Deity	Roman Deity
Sunday	Sunna	Sol Invictus
Monday	Manni	Luna
Tuesday	Tiw	Mars
Wednesday	Woden	Mercury
Thursday	Thor	Jupiter
Friday	Frigga	Venus
Saturday	n/a	Saturn

Figure 2 - Days & Deities

Holidays

Yet another legacy resides in many of our modern holidays, which began as Pagan festivals, and were co-opted by the Christian church to make it easier to assimilate new converts. The following are the three likely to be most familiar to you.

Yule (Christmas)

Yule or Yule-tide, is a winter festival that was initially celebrated by the historical Germanic peoples as a pagan religious festival, which was later absorbed into, and equated with, the Christian festival of Christmas. The festival was originally celebrated from late December to early January on a date determined by the lunar Germanic calendar. The festival was placed on December 25 when the Christian calendar (Julian calendar) was adopted. Some

7

historians claim that the celebration is connected to the Wild Hunt or was influenced by Saturnalia, the Roman winter festival.

Terms with an etymological equivalent to "Yule" are still used in the Nordic Countries for the Christian Christmas, but also for other religious holidays of the season. In modern times this has gradually led to a more secular tradition under the same name as Christmas. Yule is also used to a lesser extent in English-speaking countries to refer to Christmas. Customs such as the Yule log, Yule goat, Yule boar, Yule singing, and others stem from Yule. In modern times, Yule is observed as a cultural festival and also with religious rites by some Christians and by some Neopagans.

Ostara (Easter)

Old English Ēostre (also Ēastre) and Old High German **Ostara,** are the names of a Germanic goddess whose Anglo-Saxon month, Ēostur-monath, has given its name to the Christian festival of **Easter**. Eostre is attested by Bede, in his 8th century work *De temporum ratione*, where he states that Ēostur-monath was the equivalent to the month of April, and that feasts held in her honor during Ēostur-monath had died out by the time of his writing, replaced by the "Paschal month."

Samhain (Halloween)

Samhain marked the end of the harvest, the end of the "lighter half" of the year and beginning of the "darker half". It was traditionally celebrated over the course of several days. Many scholars believe that it was the beginning of the Celtic year. It has some elements of a festival of the dead, and the Gaels believed that the border between this world and the otherworld became thin on Samhain; because some animals and plants were dying, it thus allowed the dead to reach back through the veil that separated them from the living. Bonfires played a large part in the festivities and people and their livestock would often walk between two bonfires as a cleansing ritual, and the bones of slaughtered livestock were cast into its flames.

The Gaelic custom of wearing costumes and masks, was an attempt to copy the spirits or placate them. In Scotland the dead were impersonated by young men with masked, veiled or blackened faces, dressed in white. Samhnag — turnips which were hollowed-out and carved with faces to make lanterns — were also used to ward off harmful spirits.

The Gaelic festival became associated with the Christian All Saints' Day and All Souls' Day, and has hugely influenced the secular customs now connected with Halloween, a name first attested in the 16th century as a Scottish shortening of the fuller All-Hallows-Even. Samhain continues to be celebrated as a religious festival by some Neopagans.

Our Forebearers

In Northern Lore, we'll explore traditions and knowledge inspired by our Germanic, or Teutonic ancestors, from what is today, Northern and Western Europe – known in sagas and tales as Midgard (the middle garden). As an organic system, lore grows and evolves with time, so we'll also explore modern interpretations, and practices.

For the purposes of our journey together, lets define a few boundaries:

Northern and Western Europe will include the United Kingdom and Ireland; the northern and western parts of France and Germany, Belgium, the Netherlands, Luxembourg, Denmark, Iceland, Norway and their associated territories which include the Faroe Islands, Greenland, Svalbard and Åland. Broadly speaking, it represents the area whose climate and biogeography is significantly modified by the Gulf Stream.

Linguistically, "North-West Europe" consists of Celtic Europe and Germanic Europe, sharing some cultural traits (for example, a history of Protestantism and Germanic languages) that differentiate them from their Mediterranean Latin or Eastern European Slavic fellow-Europeans. This leads to much the same definition as the geographical one above, but would more definitely exclude France and southern Belgium. It would therefore be closer to the area normally defined as Northern Europe, excluding the Baltic and Finland.

Temporally, we'll loosely bound our exploration of the origins of the Lore starting around the time the Romans withdrew from Britain (about 410 CE) to the Norman Conquest of Britain in 1066 CE; I may color outside the lines occasionally. This period used to be referred to as the "Dark Ages" but is now more accurately described as the "Early Middle Ages". I will also include modern interpretations and synthesis of that Lore as it is practiced today.

A detailed history of all the tribes and movements of our folk is well beyond the scope of this book, however I do need to provide you an overview and timeline – a framework if you will.

We'll begin with a quick look at some of the major contributors.

Figure 3 - Midgard

The Romans

Period of Influence: 500 BCE ~ 450 CE

Cultural Impacts: Roads, Law[2], Spread of Roman Culture and Christianity

Notable Persons: Julius Ceasar, Augustus Caesar (First Emperor)

The Roman Empire at its greatest extent under Trajan in AD 117.

Figure 4 - Roman Empire

Ancient Rome was a civilization that grew out of a small agricultural community founded on the Italian Peninsula as early as the 10th century BCE. Located along the Mediterranean Sea; it became one of the largest empires in the ancient world.

---

[2] SPQR is an initialism from a Latin phrase, 'Senatus Populusque Romanus' ("The Senate and the People of Rome"), referring to the government of the ancient Roman Republic, and used as an official signature of the government. It appears on coins, at the end of documents made public, by inscription in stone or metal, in dedications of monuments and public works, and was emblazoned on the standards of the Roman legions.

The American magazine National Geographic described the legacy of the Roman Empire in The World According to Rome:

The enduring Roman influence is reflected pervasively in contemporary language, literature, legal codes, government, architecture, engineering, medicine, sports, arts, etc. Much of it is so deeply inbedded that we barely notice our debt to ancient Rome. Consider language, for example. Fewer and fewer people today claim to know Latin — and yet, go back to the first sentence in this paragraph. If we removed all the words drawn directly from Latin, that sentence would read; "The."

The Empire contributed many things to the world, such as a calendar with leap years, aspects of modern neo-classicistic and Byzantine architecture, and an extensive system of roads constructed by the Roman Army that lasts to this day. Even modern astrology comes to us directly from the Romans.

Figure 5 - Surviving Roman road in Britain

The Roman Empire also contributed its form of government, which influences various constitutions including those of most European countries and many former European colonies. In the United States, for example, the framers of the Constitution remarked, in creating the Presidency, that they wanted to inaugurate an "Augustan Age". The modern world also inherited legal thinking from Roman law, fully codified in Late Antiquity. Governing a vast territory, the Romans developed the science of public administration to an extent never before conceived or necessary, creating an extensive civil service and formalized methods of tax collection.

In about 410CE, Rome had withdrawn from Britain, and reduced its forces in much of Gaul (modern France and Western Germany).

There are many theories about why the Roman Empire began its decline, but suffice to say that a combination of factors, including political strife and pressure from invaders contributed.

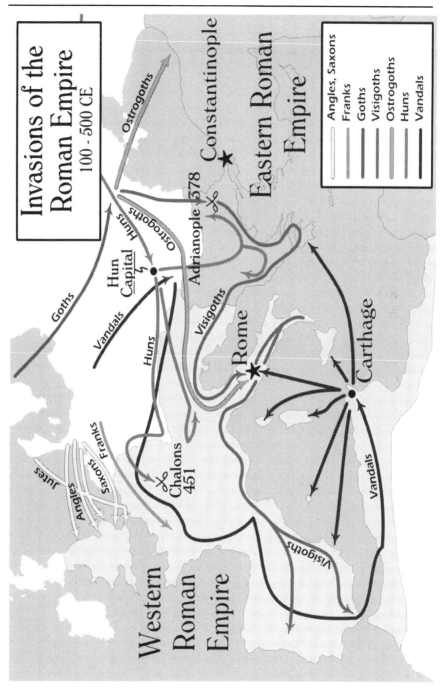

Figure 6 - Invasions of the Roman Empire

The Anglo-Saxons

Period of Influence: 450 CE ~ 900 CE

Cultural Impacts: Re-unification of British Kingdoms, Documented British History[3]

Notable Persons: Hengist and Horsa, King Rædwald, Alfred the Great

Figure 7 - Helm from the Sutton Hoo burial, possibly belonging to King Rædwald

As the Romans withdrew from Britain in the 5th century, a power vacuum remained that created the perfect opportunity for continental tribes to come and take root. After centuries of occupation, the local Britons had little military capability, and were essentially defenseless.

Migration of Germanic[4] peoples to Britain from what is now northern Germany and southern Scandinavia began in the 5th century.

Much of what we know of the movement of these Germanic Tribes to Britain comes from the ***Anglo-Saxon Chronicle***[5], which is a collection of annals in Old English chronicling the history of the Anglo-Saxons.

In the following excerpt from the Anglo-Saxon Chronicle we learn how the Germanic tribes were invited by the Britons to fight against the Picts from the North, after their pleas to Rome for assistance went unheeded.

---

[3] Possibly at the behest of Alfred the Great

[4] Angles, Saxons, and Jutes, may also have included Frisians and Franks.

[5] The annals were initially created late in the 9th century, probably in Wessex, during the reign of Alfred the Great. Multiple manuscript copies were made and distributed to monasteries across England and were independently updated.

A.D. 443. *This year sent the Britons over sea to Rome, and begged assistance against the Picts; but they had none, for the Romans were at war with Atila, king of the Huns. Then sent they to the Angles, and requested the same from the nobles of that nation.*

A.D. 449. *This year Marcian and Valentinian assumed the empire, and reigned seven winters.*

In their days Hengist and Horsa, invited by Wurtgern, king of the Britons to his assistance, landed in Britain in a place that is called Ipwinesfleet; first of all to support the Britons, but they afterwards fought against them. The king directed them to fight against the Picts; and they did so; and obtained the victory wheresoever they came.

They then sent to the Angles, and desired them to send more assistance. They described the worthlessness of the Britons, and the richness of the land. They then sent them greater support.

Then came the men from three powers of Germany; the Old Saxons, the Angles, and the Jutes.

From the Jutes are descended the men of Kent, the Wightwarians (that is, the tribe that now dwelleth in the Isle of Wight), and that kindred in Wessex that men yet call the kindred of the Jutes.

From the Old Saxons came the people of Essex and Sussex and Wessex.

From Anglia, which has ever since remained waste between the Jutes and the Saxons, came the East Angles, the Middle Angles, the Mercians, and all of those north of the Humber. Their leaders were two brothers, Hengest and Horsa; who were the sons of Wihtgils; Wihtgils was the son of Witta, Witta of Wecta, Wecta of Woden. From this Woden [Odin] arose all our royal kindred, and that of the Southumbrians also.

Upon witnessing the bounty of Britain, and it's defenseless state, the mercenaries invited the Angles, Saxons and Jutes to help them claim the land.

By around 800 CE, seven major Kingdoms had formed:

- Wessex
- East Anglia
- Mercia
- Northumbria
- Kent
- Sussex
- Essex

Figure 8 - Seven Kingdoms

One of the most prominent figures of the 9th century was **Alfred[6] the Great** (849 – 899), King of Wessex from 871 to 899. Alfred is noted for his defense of the Anglo-Saxon kingdoms of southern England against the Vikings, becoming the only English king to be accorded the epithet "the Great". Alfred was the first King of the West Saxons to style himself "King of the Anglo-Saxons". Details of his life are described in a work by the Welsh scholar and bishop, Asser. Alfred was a learned man who encouraged education and improved his kingdom's legal system and military structure. Alfred is a Catholic and an Eastern Orthodox Church saint, and is commonly regarded as a hero of the Christian Church in the Anglican Communion, with a feast day of 26 October.

---

[6] Old English:elf advice

Figure 9 - KING ALFRED THE GREAT

The Vikings

Period of Influence: 790 CE ~ 1100 CE

Cultural Impacts: Viking Raids, Discovery of America, Spread knowledge of Scandinavian Runes and other Northern Lore

Notable Persons: Eric the Red, Leif Ericsson

A Viking is one of the Norse (Scandinavian) explorers, warriors, merchants, and pirates who raided and colonized wide areas of Europe from the late eighth to the early eleventh century. These Norsemen used their famed **longships** to travel as far east as Constantinople and the Volga River in Russia, and as far west as Iceland, Greenland, and Newfoundland.

The period from the earliest recorded raids in the 790s until the Norman Conquest of England in 1066 is commonly known as the Viking Age of Scandinavia, and forms a major part of the medieval history of Scandinavia, Britain, Ireland and the rest of Europe in general.

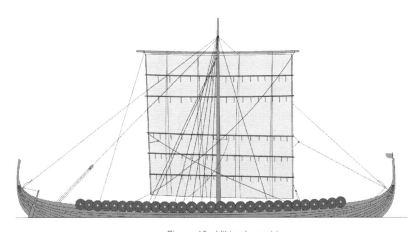

Figure 10 - Viking Longship

The Normans were descended from Danish Vikings who were given feudal over lordship of areas in northern France — the

Duchy of Normandy — in the 10th century, so in that respect, descendants of the Vikings continued to have an influence in northern Europe. Likewise, King Harold Godwinson, the last Anglo-Saxon king of England who was killed during the Norman invasion in 1066, had Danish ancestors. Many of the medieval kings of Norway and Denmark married into English and Scottish royalty and occasionally got involved in dynastic disputes.

Geographically, a "Viking Age" may be assigned not only to Scandinavian lands (modern Denmark, Norway and Sweden), but also to territories under North Germanic dominance, mainly the Danelaw, formerly the Kingdom of Northumbria, parts of Mercia, and East Anglia.

The Vikings sailed most of the North Atlantic, reaching south to North Africa and east to Russia, Constantinople and the middle east; they came as looters, traders, colonists, and mercenaries. Vikings under Leif Eriksson, heir to Erik the Red, reached North America and set up a short-lived settlement in present-day L'Anse aux Meadows, Newfoundland and Labrador, Canada.

Viking navigators opened the road to new lands to the north, west and east, resulting in the foundation of independent settlements in the Shetland, Orkney, and Faroe Islands; Iceland; Greenland; and L'Anse aux Meadows. Many of these lands, specifically Greenland and Iceland, may have been originally discovered by sailors blown off course. They also may well have been deliberately sought out, perhaps on the basis of the accounts of sailors who had seen land in the distance. The Greenland settlement eventually died out, possibly due to climate change.

Vikings also explored and settled in territories in Slavic-dominated areas of Eastern Europe, particularly the Kievan Rus. By 950CE these settlements were largely Slavicized.

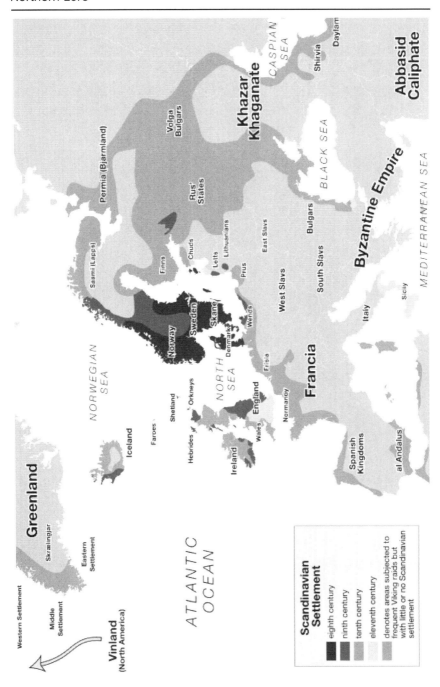

Figure 11 – Scandinavian (Viking) Settlements.

From 839, Varangian mercenaries in the service of the Byzantine Empire, notably Harald Hardrada, campaigned in North Africa, Jerusalem, and other places in the Middle East. Important trading ports during the period include Birka, Hedeby, Kaupang, Jorvik, Staraya Ladoga, Novgorod and Kiev.

Figure 12 - A reconstructed Viking Age long house

There is archaeological evidence that Vikings reached the city of Baghdad, the center of the Islamic Empire. The Norse regularly plied the Volga with their trade goods: furs, tusks, seal fat for boat sealant and slaves. However, they were far less successful in establishing settlements in the Middle East, possibly due to the more centralized Islamic power.

Generally speaking, the Norwegians expanded to the north and west to places such as Ireland, Iceland and Greenland; the Danes to England and France, settling in the Danelaw (northern/eastern England) and Normandy; and the Swedes to the east. These nations, although distinct, were similar in culture and language. The names of Scandinavian kings are known only for the later part of the Viking Age. Only after the end of the Viking Age did the separate kingdoms acquire distinct identities as nations, which went hand in hand with their Christianization. Thus the end of the Viking Age for the Scandinavians also marks the start of their relatively brief Middle Ages.

The motives driving the Viking expansion form a topic of much debate in Northern history. One common theory posits that the Norse population had outgrown the agricultural potential of their Scandinavian homeland. Although possessed of vast, uncultivated forest areas on the interior of the Scandinavian Peninsula, sea raiding was easier than clearing large areas of forest for farm and pasture in a region with a limited growing season; for a coastal population with superior naval technologies, it made sense to expand overseas in the face of a growing population.

Another explanation is that the Vikings exploited a moment of weakness in the surrounding regions. For example, the Danish Vikings were aware of the internal divisions within Charlemagne's empire that began in the 830s and resulted in schism. England suffered from internal division and was relatively easy prey given the proximity of many towns to the sea or navigable rivers. Lack of organized naval opposition throughout Western Europe allowed Viking ships to travel freely, raiding or trading as opportunity permitted.

The decline in the profitability of old trade routes could also have played a role. Trade between western Europe and the rest of Eurasia suffered a severe blow when the Roman Empire fell in the 5th century. The expansion of Islam in the 7th century had also affected trade with western Europe. Trade on the Mediterranean Sea was historically at its lowest level when the Vikings initiated their expansion. By opening new trade routes in Arabic and Frankish lands, the Vikings profited from international trade by expanding beyond their traditional boundaries. Finally, the destruction of the Frisian fleet by the Franks afforded the Vikings an opportunity to take over their trade markets.

Figure 13 - Leif Ericsson Statue, Reykjavik

Following a period of thriving trade and Viking settlement, cultural impulses flowed from the rest of Europe to affect Viking dominance. Christianity had an early and growing presence in Scandinavia, and with the rise of centralized authority and the development of more robust coastal defense systems, Viking raids became more risky and less profitable.

Snorri Sturluson in the saga of St. Olaf chapter 73, describes the brutal process of Christianization in Norway:

"...those who did not give up paganism were banished, with others he (Saint Olaf) cut off their hands or their feet or extirpated their eyes, others he ordered hanged or decapitated, but did not leave unpunished any of those who did not want to serve God (...) he afflicted them with great punishments (...) He gave them clerks and instituted some in the districts."

As the new quasi-feudalistic system became entrenched in Scandinavian rule, organized opposition sealed the Vikings' fate. Eleventh-century chronicles note Scandinavian attempts to combat the Vikings from the eastern shores of the Baltic Sea, which eventually led to Danish and Swedish participation in the Baltic Crusades during the 12th and 13th centuries. It also contributed to the development of the Hanseatic League.

One of the primary profit centers of Viking trade was slavery, and since the Church took a position that Christians should not own fellow Christians as slaves, chattel slavery diminished as a practice throughout Northern Europe. Eventually, outright slavery was outlawed, replaced with serfdom at the bottom rung of Medieval society. This took much of the economic incentive out of raiding, though sporadic activity continued for a few decades beyond the Norman conquest of England.

Figure 14 - Statue of Three Viking Swords at Hafrsfjord Norway

The Normans

Period of Influence: 911 CE ~ 1200 CE
Cultural Impacts: Conquest of Britain, Massive Cultural Shift

Interesting Figures: William the Conqueror, Duke of Normandy

The Normans gave their name to Normandy, a region in northern France; they were descended from Viking conquerors/settlers of the territory and the native population of mostly Frankish and Gallo-Roman stock. Their identity emerged initially in the first half of the tenth century, and gradually evolved over succeeding centuries until they disappeared as an ethnic group in the early thirteenth century. The name "Normans" derives from "Northmen" or "Norsemen", after the Vikings from Scandinavia who founded Normandy.

They played a major political, military, and cultural role in medieval Europe and even the Near East. They were famed for their martial spirit and Christian piety. They quickly adopted the Romance language of the land they settled in, their dialect becoming known as Norman, an important literary language. The Duchy of Normandy, which they formed by treaty with the French crown, was one of the great large fiefs of medieval France. The Normans are famed both for their culture, such as their unique Romanesque architecture, and their musical traditions, as well as for their military accomplishments and innovations. Norman adventurers established a kingdom in Sicily and southern Italy by conquest, and a Norman expedition on behalf of their duke led to the Norman Conquest of England. Norman influence spread from these new centers to the Crusader States in the Near East, to Scotland and Wales in Great Britain, and to Ireland.

The Normans were in contact with England from an early date. Not only were their original Viking brethren still ravaging the English coasts, they occupied most of the important ports opposite England across the Channel. This relationship eventually produced closer ties of blood through the marriage of Emma, sister of Duke Richard II of Normandy, and King Ethelred II of England. Because of this, Ethelred fled to Normandy in 1013, when he was forced from his kingdom by Sweyn Forkbeard. His stay in Normandy (until 1016) influenced him and his sons by Emma, who stayed in Normandy after Canute the Great's conquest of the isle.

Figure 15 - Bayeux Tapestry

The Norman conquest of England began in 1066 with the invasion of the Kingdom of England by the troops of William, Duke of Normandy, and his victory at the Battle of Hastings.

The Norman Conquest was a pivotal event in English history for several reasons. It largely removed the native ruling class, replacing it with a foreign, French-speaking monarchy, aristocracy, and clerical hierarchy. This, in turn, brought about a transformation of the English language and the culture of England.

By subjecting the country to rulers originating in France it linked England more closely with continental Europe, while lessening Scandinavian influence, and set the stage for a rivalry with France that would continue intermittently for many centuries. It also had important consequences for the rest of the British Isles, paving the way for further Norman conquests in Wales and Ireland, and the extensive penetration of the aristocracy of Scotland by Norman and other French-speaking families, with the accompanying spread of continental institutions and cultural influences.

The invading Normans and their descendants replaced the Anglo-Saxons as the ruling class of England. The nobility of England were part of a single French-speaking culture and many had lands on both sides of the channel. Early Norman kings of England were, as Dukes of Normandy, vassals to the King of France. They may not have necessarily considered England to be their most important holding (although it brought the title of King - an important status symbol). King Richard I (the Lionheart) is often thought to epitomize a medieval English King, but he only spoke French and spent more time in Aquitaine or on Crusade than in England.

Eventually, the Normans merged with the natives, combining languages and traditions. In the course of the Hundred Years war, the Norman aristocracy often identified themselves as English. The Anglo-Norman language became distinct from the French language, something that was the subject of some humor by Geoffrey Chaucer. The Anglo-Norman language was eventually absorbed into the English language of their subjects and influenced it, helping (along with the Norse language of the earlier Anglo-Norse settlers and the Latin used by the church) the development of Middle English which would gain much vocabulary of French origin.

Figure 16 - William The Conqueror

Ever Onward

I hope you're now intrigued by the vast and exciting body of history we've inherited. What we've shared are just a few snapshots of an overall story that spans centuries. The most exciting part in my opinion, is that once you know where to start looking, you can find evidence of our cultural treasures lurking everywhere, from days of the week, holidays, place names and more - Keep digging!

Let's take a deeper look into some fascinating cultural treasures and manifestations.

Chapter 2 - Runes

Rūn – Old English, meaning secret

he word runes, for many, conjures up images of Tolkien's "The Hobbit", with dwarves, dragons and magical rings; after reading the book, I remember fondly learning how to write my name in (what I would later learn were) Anglo-Saxon runes. At the time they seemed like fanciful characters, and I was delighted to use them purely for aesthetic reasons – sketching in my school notebooks and such. Little did I know that 1500 years earlier, my ancestors used them daily, not only for writing, but also for magical and divinatory purposes. There is a good body of knowledge for both the exoteric, and esoteric aspects of the runes – in this chapter we will cover only the exoteric[7] aspects, such as their history, use in writing, for monuments etc.

So what are Runes? A runic row is a form of alphabet, which itself is a standardized set of letters — basic written symbols or graphemes[8] — each of which roughly represents a phoneme[9] in a spoken language, either as it exists now, or as it was in the past.

The runes were used to write various Germanic languages prior to the adoption of the Latin alphabet, and for specialized

---

[7] See Chapter 9 – Spiritual Practices for esoteric meanings and uses.

[8] A grapheme (from the Greek: γράφω, gráphō, "write") is a fundamental unit in a written language.

[9] In a language or dialect, a phoneme (from the Greek: φώνημα, phōnēma, "a sound uttered") is the smallest segmental unit of sound employed to form meaningful contrasts between utterances.

purposes thereafter. The Scandinavian variants are also known as futhark (or fuþark, derived from their first six letters of the alphabet[10]: F, U, Þ, A, R, and K); the Anglo-Saxon variant is futhorc (due to sound changes undergone in Old English).

The origins of the runic alphabet are uncertain, although many characters of the Elder Futhark bear a close resemblance to characters from the Latin alphabet. Other candidates are the 5th to 1st century BC Northern Italic alphabets: Lepontic, Rhaetic and Venetic, all of which are closely related to each other and descend from the Old Italic alphabet.

The runes were in use among the Germanic peoples from the 1st or 2nd century CE. This period corresponds to the late Common Germanic stage linguistically, with a continuum of dialects not yet clearly separated into the three branches of later centuries; North Germanic, West Germanic, and East Germanic.

The name runes contrasts with Latin or Greek letters. It is attested on a 6th century Alamannic runestaff as runa, and possibly as runo on the 4th century Einang stone. The name is from a root run- (Gothic runa), meaning "secret" or "whisper".

The earliest runic inscriptions date from around 150 CE, and the characters were generally replaced by the Latin alphabet along with Christianization by around 700 CE in central Europe, and by around 1100 CE in Northern Europe; however, the use of runes persisted for specialized purposes in Northern Europe, longest in rural Sweden, until the early twentieth century (used mainly for decoration as runes in Dalarna and on Runic calendars).

---

[10] The word "alphabet" came into Middle English from the Late Latin word Alphabetum, which in turn originated in the Ancient Greek Alphabetos, from alpha and beta, the first two letters of the Greek alphabet.

The three best-known runic rows, and their approximate years of common usage are:

- **Elder Futhark** (around 150 to 800 CE),
- **Old English Futhorc** (400 to 1100 CE),
- **Younger Futhark** (800–1100 CE).

Figure 17 - Antler Comb

A comb made of antler from around 150 to 200 CE and was found in Vimose on the island of Funen, Denmark. The Elder Futhark inscription reads "Harja", a male name. This is the oldest known runic inscription. The comb is housed at the National Museum of Denmark.

Elder Futhark

The Elder Futhark is the oldest form of the runic row, used by Germanic tribes for Northwest Germanic and Migration period Germanic dialects of the 2nd to 8th centuries for inscriptions on artifacts such as jewellery, amulets, tools, weapons and runestones. In Scandinavia, the script was simplified to the Younger Futhark from the late 8th century, while the Anglo-Saxons and Frisians extended the Futhark which eventually became the Anglo-Saxon futhorc.

Unlike the Younger Futhark, which remained in use until modern times, the knowledge of how to read the Elder Futhark was forgotten, and it was not until 1865 that the Norwegian scholar Sophus Bugge managed to decipher it.

The Elder Futhark consists of 24 runes that are arranged in three groups of eight; each group is referred to as an Ætt. The earliest known sequential listing of the full set of 24 runes dates to around 400 AD and is found on the Kylver Stone in Gotland, Sweden.

Figure 18 - Kylver Stone

Each rune most probably had a name, chosen to represent the sound of the rune itself. The names are, however, not directly attested for the Elder Futhark themselves. Reconstructed names in Proto-Germanic have been produced, based on the names given for the runes in the later alphabets attested in the rune poems and the linked names of the letters of the Gothic alphabet.

Elder Rune	Germanic Name	Meaning
ᚠ	Fehu	Cattle, Portable Wealth
ᚢ	Uruz	Aurochs
ᚦ	Thurisaz	Giant
ᚨ	Ansuz	A god
ᚱ	Raido	Riding
ᚲ	Kenaz	Torch, light
ᚷ	Gebo	Gift
ᚹ	Wunjo	Joy
ᚺ	Hagalaz	Hail
ᚾ	Nauthiz	Need
ᛁ	Isa	Ice
ᛃ	Jera	Year, harvest
ᛇ	Eihwaz	Yew
ᛈ	Pertho	Birth, chance
ᛉ	Algiz	Protection
ᛋ	Sowilo	Sun
ᛏ	Teiwaz	the god Tyr
ᛒ	Berkana	Birch (or Poplar)
ᛖ	Ehwaz	Horse
ᛗ	Mannaz	Man
ᛚ	Laguz	Water, lake
ᛜ	Inguz	the god Freyr
ᛞ	Dagaz	Day
ᛟ	Othila	Inherited land

Anglo-Saxon Futhorc.

The Anglo-Saxon Futhorc was descended from the Elder Futhark of 24 runes and contained between 26 and 33 characters. It was used probably from the fifth century onward, for recording Old English and Old Frisian.

Figure 19 - 7'th c. Franks Casket

The front panel of the 7th century Franks Casket, depicting the Germanic legend of Weyland Smith and containing a riddle in Anglo-Saxon runes. Note how runes are written left to right at the top, and right to left at the bottom.

There are competing theories as to the origins of the Anglo-Saxon futhorc. One theory proposes that it was developed in Frisia and from there spread later to England. Another holds that runes were first introduced to England from Scandinavia where the futhorc was modified and then exported to Frisia.

The early futhorc was identical to the Elder Futhark except for the split of ᚠ a into three variants ᚪ āc, ᚫ æsc and ᚩ ōs, resulting in 26 runes. The earliest ᚩ ōs rune is found on the 5th century Undley bracteate. ᚪ āc was introduced later, in the 6th century. The double-barred ᚻ hægl characteristic for continental inscriptions is first attested as late as 698, on St. Cuthbert's coffin; before that, the single-barred Scandinavian variant was used.

In England the futhorc was further extended to 28 and finally to 33 runes, and runic writing in England became closely associated with the Latin scriptoria from the time of Anglo-Saxon Christianization in the 7th century.

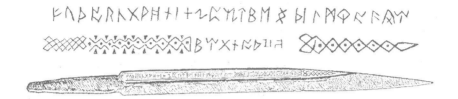

Figure 20 - Thames Scaramasax

The Thames scramasax is a 9th century weapon, recovered from the Thames at Battersea, London. It bears a Futhorc inscription. The row of 28 runes; This is the only known epigraphical example of the 28 Anglos-Saxon futhorc row. In addition to the futhorc, the name Beagnoþ is inscribed: ᛒᛠᚷᚾᚩᚦ

The futhorc started to be replaced by the Latin alphabet from around the 9th century. In some cases, texts would be written in the Latin alphabet but runes would be used in place of the word it represented, and the runes þorn (Þ, þ) and wynn (Ƿ, ƿ, ƿ)came to be used as extensions of the Latin alphabet. By the Norman Conquest of 1066 CE it was very rare and disappeared altogether shortly thereafter. From at least five centuries of use, fewer than 200 artifacts bearing futhorc inscriptions have survived. The futhorc is an extended alphabet, consisting of 29, and later even 33 characters; it was probably used from the 5th century onward. There are competing theories as to the origins of the Anglo-Saxon Fuþorc. One theory proposes that it was developed in Frisia and later spread to England. Another holds that runes were introduced by Scandinavians to England where the fuþorc was modified and exported to Frisia. Both theories have their inherent weaknesses and a definitive answer likely awaits more archaeological evidence.

The Anglo-Saxon rune poem lists the following characters and names:

ᚠ feoh, ᚢ ur, ᚦ thorn, ᚩ os, ᚱ rad, ᚲ cen, ᚷ gyfu, ᚹ wynn, ᚻ haegl, ᚾ nyd, ᛁ is, ᛄ ger, ᛇ eoh, ᛈ peordh, ᛉ eolh, ᛋ sigel, ᛏ tir, ᛒ beorc, ᛗ eh, ᛗ mann, ᛚ lagu, ᛝ ing, ᛟ ethel, ᛞ daeg, ᚪ ac, ᚫ aesc, ᚣ yr, ᛠ ior, ᛠ ear.

The expanded alphabet features the additional letters ᛢ cweorth, ᛣ calc, ᛤ cealc and ᛥ stan- these additional letters have only been found in manuscripts. Feoh, þorn, and sigel stood for [f], [þ], and [s] in most environments, but voiced to [v], [ð], and [z] between vowels or voiced consonants. Gyfu and wynn stood for the letters yogh and wynn, which became [g] and [w] in Middle English.

Younger Futhark

The Younger Futhark, also called Scandinavian runes, is a reduced form of the Elder Futhark, consisting of only 16 characters, in use from ca. 800 CE. The reduction, paradoxically, happened at the same time as phonetic changes led to a greater number of different phonemes in the spoken language, when Proto-Norse evolved into Old Norse.

Thus, the language included distinct sounds and minimal pairs which were not separate in writing. Also, since the writing custom avoided having the same rune twice in consecutive order, the spoken distinction between long and short vowels were not retained in writing, either. The only real reason for using the same rune consecutively, would be when it represented different sounds following each other.

Usage of the Younger Futhark is found in Scandinavia and Viking Age settlements abroad, probably in use from the 9th century onward. While the Migration Period Elder Futhark had been an actual "secret" known only to a literate elite, with only some 350 surviving inscriptions, literacy in the Younger Futhark became widespread in Scandinavia, as witnessed by the great number of

Runestones (some 6,000), sometimes inscribed with almost casual notes.

The Younger Futhark became known in Europe as the "alphabet of the Norsemen", and was studied in the interest of trade and diplomatic contacts, referred to as Abecedarium Nordmannicum in Frankish Fulda (possibly by Walahfrid Strabo) and *ogam lochlannach* "Ogham[11] of the Scandinavians" in the Book of Ballymote.

The Younger Futhark is divided into long-branch (Danish) and short-twig (Swedish and Norwegian) runes. The difference between the two versions has been a matter of controversy. A general opinion is that the difference was functional, i.e. the long-branch runes were used for documentation on stone, whereas the short-branch runes were in everyday use for private or official messages on wood. In addition the **Hälsinge Runes** (staveless runes, ca. 900–1200), **Middle Age runes** (ca. 1100–1500) and the Latinized **Dalecarlian futhark** (ca. 1500–1910) were developed out of the Younger futhark.

The Icelandic and Norwegian rune poems list 16 runes, with the stave names:

ᚠ fe ("wealth"), ᚢ ur ("iron"/"rain"), ᚦ Thurs ("giant"), ᚬ As/Oss, ᚱ reidh ("ride"), ᚴ kaun ("ulcer"), ᚼ hagall ("hail"), ᚾ naudhr/naud ("need"), ᛁ is/iss ("ice"), ᛅ ar ("plenty"), ᛋ sol ("sun"), ᛏ Tyr, ᛒ bjarkan/bjarken ("birch"), ᛘ madhr/madr ("man"), ᛚ logr/lög ("water"), ᛦ yr ("yew").

---

[11] Ogham is an Early Medieval alphabet used primarily to write the Old Irish language, and occasionally the Brythonic language. Ogham is sometimes referred to as the "Celtic Tree Alphabet", based on a High Medieval Bríatharogam tradition ascribing names of trees to the individual letters.

An inscription
using cipher runes,
the Elder Futhark
and the Younger
Futhark, on the
9th century Rök
Runestone in
Sweden.

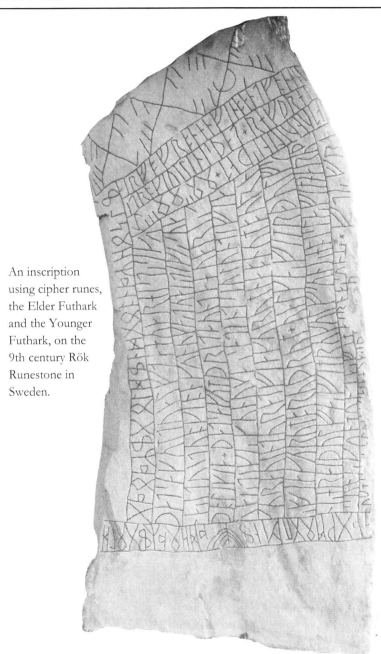

Figure 21 - Rök Runestone

Long-branch runes

The long-branch runes were rendered as follows:

ᚠᚢᚦᚨᚱᚴᚺᚾᛁᛆᛋᛏᛒᛘᛚᛦ

f u þ ą r k h n i a s t b m l ʀ

Short-twig runes

In the short-twig runes (or Rök runes), nine runes appear as simplified variants of the long-branch runes, while the remaining seven have identical shapes:

ᚠᚢᚦᚨᚱᚴᚼᚾᛁ ᛆᛋᛐᛒᛘ ᛚᛦ

f u þ ą r k h n i a s t b m l ʀ

Hälsinge Runes (staveless runes)

Hälsinge runes are so named because in modern times they were first noticed in the Hälsingland region of Sweden. Later other runic inscriptions with the same runes were found in other parts of Sweden. They were used between the 10th and 12th centuries. The runes seem to be a simplification of the Swedish-Norwegian runes and lack vertical strokes, hence the name 'staveless.' They cover the same set of staves as the other Younger Futhark alphabets.

Medieval Runes

In the Middle Ages, the Younger Futhark in Scandinavia was expanded, so that it once more contained one sign for each phoneme of the old Norse language. Dotted variants of voiceless signs were introduced to denote the corresponding voiced consonants, or vice versa, voiceless variants of voiced consonants, and several new runes also appeared for vowel sounds. Inscriptions in medieval Scandinavian runes show a large number of variant rune-forms, and some letters, such as *s*, *c* and *z*, were often used interchangeably.

abcdþðefghiklmnopqrstuvyzæø

Medieval runes were in use until the 15th century. Of the total number of Norwegian runic inscriptions preserved today, most are medieval runes. Notably, more than 600 inscriptions using these runes have been discovered in Bergen since the 1950s, mostly on wooden sticks (the so-called Bryggen inscriptions). This indicates that runes were in common use side by side with the Latin alphabet for several centuries. Indeed some of the medieval runic inscriptions are actually in Latin language.

Figure 22 - Stenkvista Runestone

Origins

The runes developed centuries after the Old Italic alphabets from which they are historically derived. The debate on the development of the runic script concerns the question which of the Italic alphabets should be taken as their point of origin, and which, if any, signs should be considered original innovations added to the letters found in the Italic scripts. The historical context of the script's origin is the cultural contact between Germanic people, who often served as mercenaries in the Roman army, and the Italic peninsula during the Roman imperial period (1st c. BC to 5th c. AD). The formation of the Elder Futhark was complete by the early 5th century, with the Kylver Stone being the first evidence of the futhark ordering as well as of the p rune.

The Raetic alphabet of Bolzano is often advanced as a candidate for the origin of the runes, with only five Elder Futhark runes (ᛖ e, ᛁ ï, ᛃ j, ᛜ ŋ, ᛈ p) having no counterpart in the Bolzano alphabet. Scandinavian scholars tend to favor derivation from the Latin alphabet itself over Raetic candidates. A "North Etruscan" thesis is supported by the inscription on the Negau helmet dating to the 2nd century BC. This is in a northern Etruscan alphabet, but features a Germanic name, **Harigast**.

The angular shapes of the runes are shared with most contemporary alphabets of the period used for carving in wood or stone. A peculiarity of the runic alphabet is the absence of horizontal strokes, although this characteristic is also shared by other alphabets, such as the early form of the Latin alphabet used for the Duenos inscription, and it is not universal especially among early runic inscriptions, which frequently have variant rune shapes including horizontal strokes.

Runes in Eddic lore

In Norse mythology, the runic alphabet is said to have a divine origin (Old Norse: reginkunnr). This is attested as early as on the Noleby Runestone from around 600 AD that reads:

Runo fahi raginakundo toj[e'k]a...,

Meaning "I prepare the suitable divine rune ..."

An attestation from the 9th century on the Sparlösa Runestone reads:

Ok rað runaR þaR rægi[n]kundu, meaning

Meaning "And interpret the runes of divine origin".

Figure 23 - Noleby Runestone

More notably, in the Poetic Edda poem Havamal[12], Stanza 80, the runes are also described as reginkunnr:

Old Norse	English
Þat er þá reynt,	*That is now proved,*
er þú að rúnum spyrr	*what you asked of the runes,*
inum reginkunnum,	*of the potent famous ones,*
þeim er gerðu ginnregin	*which the great gods made,*
ok fáði fimbulþulr,	*and the mighty sage stained,*
þá hefir hann bazt, ef hann þegir.	*that it is best for him if he stays silent.*

The poem Havamal explains that the originator of the runes was the major god Odin. Stanza 138 describes how Odin received the runes through self-sacrifice:

Old Norse	English
Veit ek at ek hekk vindga meiði a	*I know that I hung on a windy tree*
netr allar nío,	*nine long nights,*
geiri vndaþr ok gefinn Oðni,	*wounded with a spear, dedicated to Odin,*
sialfr sialfom mer,	*myself to myself,*
a þeim meiþi, er mangi veit, hvers hann	*on that tree of which no man knows*
af rótom renn.	*from where its roots run.*

---

[12] Which we'll explore in Chapter 8 – Tao

In stanza 139, Odin continues:

Old Norse	**English**
Við hleifi mik seldo ne viþ hornigi,	*No bread did they give me nor a drink*
nysta ek niþr,	*from a horn,*
nam ek vp rvnar,	*downwards I peered;*
opandi nam,	*I took up the runes,*
fell ek aptr þaðan.	*screaming I took them,*
	then I fell back from there.

In the Poetic Edda poem Rígsþula another origin is related of how the runic alphabet became known to man. The poem relates how Ríg, identified as Heimdall in the introduction, sired three sons (Thrall (slave), Churl (freeman) and Jarl (noble)) on human women. These sons became the ancestors of the three classes of men indicated by their names. When Jarl reached an age when he began to handle weapons and show other signs of nobility, Rig returned and, having claimed him as a son, taught him the runes. In 1555, the exiled Swedish archbishop Olaus Magnus recorded a tradition that a man named Kettil Runske had stolen three rune staffs from Odin and learned the runes and their magic.

J. R. R. Tolkien and contemporary fiction

In J. R. R. Tolkien's novel The Hobbit (1937), the Anglo-Saxon runes are used on a map to emphasize its connection to the Dwarves. They were also used in the initial drafts of The Lord of the Rings, but later were replaced by the Cirth, a rune-like alphabet invented by Tolkien.

Following Tolkien, historical and fictional runes appear commonly in modern popular culture, particularly in fantasy literature, video games, and various other forms of media. For example, the alien Asgard race from the science fiction television series Stargate SG-1 use runes as their written language.

Figure 24 - The Weather Peasant

Chapter 3 - Weather Lore

n this third chapter, we'll explore a sampling of the Weather Lore at our disposal. What natural phenomenon did our forefathers study and use to their advantage & why?

Modern meteorology has come a long way in the last hundred years; with the advent of weather radar to track and predict storm paths, as well as the science of climatology, and their ability to "read" the weather patterns and conditions hundreds of thousands of years into the past.

Since the dawn of time, man has had a fascination with weather, more so when he learned to sow crops; now mans existence was tied directly to weather. Given that we've been predominantly agrarian for more than 10,000 years or so, it should follow that we have a good body of experience to draw upon with regard to the observation of the weather, and understanding it's patterns and cycles. Yet in today's society, we're quick to disregard or dismiss our old proverbs and fables – but should we? I'd like to examine some of these old pieces of wisdom, and correlate them with modern meteorological evidence. Of course not all were accurate, but a surprising number are.

Introduction[13]

"The state of the weather is almost the first subject about which people talk when they meet, and it is not surprising that a

---

[13] The following Introduction, edited by the author, comes from "Weather Lore", published in 1898 by Richard Inwards.

matter of such importance to comfort, health, prosperity, and even life itself, should form the usual text and starting-point for the conversation of daily life.

From the earliest times, hunters, shepherds, sailors, and tillers of the earth have from sheer necessity been led to study the teachings of the winds, the waves, the clouds, and a hundred other objects from which the signs of coming changes in the state of the air might be foretold. The weather-wise amongst these primitive people would be naturally the most prosperous, and others would soon acquire the coveted foresight by a closer observance of the same objects from which their successful rivals guessed the proper time to provide against a storm, or reckoned on the prospects of the coming crops. The result has been the framing of a rough set of rules, and the laying down of many "wise saws[14]," about the weather, and the freaks to which it is liable. Some of these observations have settled down into the form of proverbs ; others have taken the shape of rhymes; while many are yet floating about, unclaimed and unregistered, but passed from mouth to mouth, as mere records of facts, varying in verbal form according to local idioms, but owning a common origin and purport .

Many weather proverbs contain evidence of keen observation and just reasoning, but a greater number are the offspring of the common tendency to form conclusions from a too limited observation of facts. Even those which have not been confirmed by later experience will be interesting, if only to show the errors into which men may be led by seeing Nature with eyes half closed by prejudice or superstition. It has seemed to me desirable that all this "fossil wisdom" should be collected, and I have endeavored in this book to present in a systematic form all the current weather lore which is in any way applicable to the climate of the British Isles."

"It would be strange if all the observations brought in this volume to a common focus did not cast a new ray or two of light on

---

[14] From the saying "Wise saws and modern instances" where wise saws are traditional, well understood legal rulings and modern instances are new judgments.

the point to which they have all been directed. Out of so many shots some must hit the mark, though the reader must be warned that even in this "multitude of counsel" there is not absolute safety. These predictions are, after all, but gropings in the dark; and although skilled observers, armed with the delicate instruments contrived by modern science, may be able to forecast with some success the weather for a few hours, yet with respect to the coming months and seasons, or the future harvests and vintages, <u>the learned meteorologist is only on a level with the peasant who watches from the hilltop</u> the "spreadings and driftings of the clouds," or hazards his rude weather guesses from the behavior of his cattle or the blossoming of the hedge flowers which adorn his paths."

Red Sky at Night[15]

"Red sky at night, sailor's delight.
Red sky in morning, sailor's warning"

Weather lore concerning the appearance of the sky, the conditions of the atmosphere, the type or movement of the clouds, and the direction of the winds may have a scientific basis and likely can predict the weather.

Shakespeare said something similar in his play, Venus and Adonis.

"Like a red morn that ever yet betokened, Wreck to the seaman, tempest to the field, Sorrow to the shepherds, woe unto the birds, Gusts and foul flaws to herdmen and to herds."

In the Bible, (Matthew XVI: 2-3,) Jesus said,

"When in evening, ye say, it will be fair weather: For the sky is red. And in the morning, it will be foul weather today; for the sky is red and lowering."

---

[15] Article from the Library of Congress website www.loc.gov

In order to understand why "Red sky at night, sailor's delight. Red sky in morning, sailor's warning" can predict the weather, we must understand more about weather and the colors in the sky. Usually, weather moves from west to east, blown by the westerly trade winds. This means storm systems generally move in from the West.

The colors we see in the sky are due to the rays of sunlight being split into colors of the spectrum as they pass through the atmosphere and ricochet off the water vapor and particles in the atmosphere. The amounts of water vapor and dust particles in the atmosphere are good indicators of weather conditions. They also determine which colors we will see in the sky.

During sunrise and sunset the sun is low in the sky, and it transmits light through the thickest part of the atmosphere. A red sky suggests an atmosphere loaded with dust and moisture particles. We see the red, because red wavelengths (the longest in the color spectrum) are breaking through the atmosphere. The shorter wavelengths, such as blue, are scattered and broken up.

Red sky at night, sailors delight.

When we see a red sky at night, this means that the setting sun is sending its light through a high concentration of dust particles. This usually indicates high pressure and stable air coming in from the west. Basically good weather will follow.

Red sky in morning, sailor's warning.

A red sunrise reflects the dust particles of a system that has just passed from the west. This indicates that a storm system may be moving to the east. If the morning sky is a deep fiery red, it means a high water content in the atmosphere. So, rain is on its way.

Sound transmission

When sounds travel far and wide,
A stormy day will betide.

This piece of lore is true in summer but conditionally false in winter. Moisture-laden air is a better conductor of sound than dry air, so moist air carries sounds farther. In winter, temperature also becomes an important factor. If the air is warm and moist, the rule holds. If the air is very cold, it is also very dense and a better sound conductor than warm air, and also likely to be much drier. When sounds carry over a long distance, the cold, clear weather is likely to linger.

Low pressure regions

Cold, blustery northerly winds typically accompany a low pressure system.

When the wind is blowing in the North
No fisherman should set forth,
When the wind is blowing in the East,
'Tis not fit for man nor beast,
When the wind is blowing in the South
It brings the food over the fish's mouth,
When the wind is blowing in the West,
That is when the fishing's best!

In western European seas, this description of wind direction is an excellent illustration of how the weather events of an active low pressure area present themselves. With the approach of a low, easterly winds typically pick up. These gusty winds can be unpleasant for a number of reasons; they are often uncomfortably warm, dry, and dusty in the summer and bitterly cold in the winter. Northerly winds, which follow around a low, are cold and blustery. Sailing in conditions of northerly winds requires expertise and a boat capable of handling heavy waves. Southerly winds usually bring warm temperatures, and though they may not necessarily feed the fish, they do provide pleasant fishing weather. The best circumstance, however, is to have a westerly wind blowing; the wind condition is likely to persist for some time, the weather should remain fair and clear, and the wind should be relatively constant.

Wind and weather observations will be different for a low passing to the north of the observer than for one passing to the south. When a low passes to the north, the winds typically pick up from the east, swing to southerly (possibly accompanied by light precipitation, usually not) with the passage of the low's warm front, and then switch to northwesterly or westerly as the cold front passes. Typically, if there is any heavy precipitation, it will accompany the passage of the cold front. When a low passes to the south, on the other hand, winds will initially pick up from the east, but will gradually shift to northerly. Overcast skies and steady precipitation often occur as the center of the low passes due south, but skies will clear and winds will gradually become westerly as the low moves off to the east. No observer will experience all the weather elements of a low in a single passage.

Calm conditions

No weather is ill, if the wind be still.

Calm conditions, especially with clear skies, indicate the dominance of a high pressure area. Because highs are broad regions of descending air, they discourage the formation of phenomena typically associated with weather, such as clouds, wind, and precipitation. Calm conditions, though, may also result from a circumstance known as "the calm before the storm," in which a large thunderstorm cell to the west may be updrafting the westerly surface wind before it can arrive locally. This situation is readily identifiable by looking to the west — such an approaching storm will be close enough to be unmistakable. In winter, though, calm air and clear skies may signal the presence of an Arctic high, typically accompanied by very cold air, and it is difficult to imagine describing a temperature of -35°C as pleasant.

Humidity indicators

When windows won't open, and the salt clogs the shaker,
The weather will favour the umbrella maker!

Moisture in the air causes wood to swell, making doors and windows sticky, and salt is a very effective absorber of moisture. With a high level of moisture in the air, the likelihood of precipitation is increased. The Sodium Iodide in iodized salt acts as an anti-clumping agent in humid conditions, leading to Morton Salt's umbrella girl logo and slogan "When it rains, it pours".

Aches and pains

A coming storm your shooting corns presage,
And aches will throb, your hollow tooth will rage.

There have been medical studies done which indicate some people experience this effect. The most likely reason is that with a fall in atmospheric pressure, blood vessels dilate slightly in reaction. This has the effect of aggravating already-irritated nerves near corns, cavities, or arthritic joints. Studies are inconclusive, however, with some researchers attributing this effect to selective memory.

Seagull forecasts

Seagull, seagull sit on the sand.
It's never good weather when you're on land.

Seagulls are not especially fond of standing or walking. They are naturally at home in flight, and where they can, they sleep on the water. However, seagulls, like people, find gusty, turbulent wind difficult to contend with, and under such circumstances, the water is also choppy and unpleasant. Seagulls huddled on the ground are not a predictor of bad weather as much as they are a sign that the weather is already bad.

A ring around the moon

When halo rings the moon or sun, rain's approaching on the run

Figure 25 - Solar halo is precursor to rain

A halo around the sun or moon is caused by the refraction of that body's light by ice crystals at high altitude. Such high-level moisture is a precursor to moisture moving in at increasingly lower levels, and is a good indicator that an active weather system is on its way. Halos typically evolve into what is known as "milk sky", when the sky appears clear, but the typical blue is either washed-out or barely noticeable. This high, thick cirrostratus cloud is a clear indicator of an approaching low.

In the coldest days of winter, a halo around the sun is evidence of very cold and typically clear air at and above the surface. But sun dogs (a luminous ring or halo on either side of the sun) are indicators that weather conditions are likely to change in the next 18 to 36 hours.

Pasture-watching

A cow with its tail to the West makes the weather best,
A cow with its tail to the East makes the weather least

Cows, like people, prefer not to have the wind blowing in their faces, and so typically stand with their backs to the wind. Since westerly winds typically mean arriving or continuing fair weather and easterly winds usually indicate arriving or continuing unsettled weather, a "cowvane" is as good a way as any of knowing what the weather will be up to for the next few hours.

Figure 26 - Highland cow in Scotland with his back to the wind

59

Fog

A summer fog for fair,
A winter fog for rain.
A fact most everywhere,
In valley or on plain.

Fog is formed when the air cools enough that the vapor pressure encourages condensation over evaporation. In order for the air to be cool on a summer night, the sky must be clear, so excess heat can be radiated into space. Cloudy skies act like a blanket, absorbing and reradiating the heat, keeping it in. So if it is cool enough (and clear enough) for fog to form, it will probably be clear the next day.

Winter fog is the result of two entirely different circumstances. Above the ocean or a large lake, air is typically more humid than above land. When the humid air moves over cold land, it will form fog and precipitation. (To the east of the North American Great Lakes, this is a common phenomenon, and is known as the "lake effect."). In northerly climates, ice fog may form when the temperature drops substantially below freezing. It is almost exclusively an urban phenomenon, when the air is so cold that any vapor pressure results in condensation, and additional vapor emitted by automobiles, household furnaces, and industrial plants simply accumulates as fog.

Cloud movement

If clouds move against the wind, rain will follow.

This rule may be true under a few special circumstances, otherwise it is false. By standing with one's back to the ground-level wind and observing the movement of the clouds, it is possible to determine whether the weather will improve or deteriorate. For the Northern Hemisphere, it works like this: If the upper-level clouds are moving from the right, a low-pressure area has passed and the weather will improve; if from the left, a low pressure area is arriving and the weather will deteriorate. (Reverse for the Southern Hemisphere.) This is known as the "crossed-winds" rule. Clouds traveling parallel to but against the wind may indicate a thunderstorm approaching. Outflow winds typically blow opposite to the updraft zone, and clouds carried in the upper level wind will appear to be moving against the surface wind. However, if such a storm is in the offing, it is not necessary to observe the cloud motions to know rain is a good possibility. The nature of airflows *directly at* a frontal boundary can also create conditions in which lower winds contradict the motions of upper clouds, and the passage of a frontal boundary is often marked by precipitation. Most often, however, this situation occurs in the lee of a low pressure area, to the north of the frontal zones and convergence region, and does not indicate a change in weather, but rather, that the weather, fair or showery, will remain so for a period of hours at least.

Special weather-forecasting days

In the British Isles, Saint Swithun's day (July 15) is said to forecast the weather for the rest of the summer. If St Swithun's day is dry, then the legend says that the next forty days will also be dry. If however it rains, the rain will continue for forty days. In France, Saint Medard (June 8), Urban of Langres, and Saint Gervase and Saint Protais (June 19) are credited with an influence on the weather almost identical with that attributed to St Swithun in England, while in Flanders there is St Godelieve (July 6) and in Germany the Seven Sleepers' day (June 27).

There is a scientific basis to the legend of St Swithun's day. Around the middle of July, the jet stream settles into a pattern which, in the majority of years, holds reasonably steady until the end of August. When the jet stream lies north of the British Isles then continental high pressure is able to move in; when it lies across or south of the British Isles, Arctic air and Atlantic weather systems predominate.

In Russia, the weather on the feast of the Protecting Veil is popularly believed to indicate the severity of the forthcoming winter. In France, besides Saint Medard (June 8), other saints associated with weather prediction included Urban of Langres, and Saint Gervase and Saint Protais (June 19). In Flanders, there is St Godelieve (July 6) and in Germany the Seven Sleepers' Day (June 27).

There was an old proverb from Romagna that ran: "Par San Paternian e' trema la coda a e' can." ("On St. Paternian's day, the dog's tail wags"). This Cervian proverb refers to the fact that the cold began to be felt around the saint's feast day. A farmers' saying associated with Quirinus' feast day of March 30 was "Wie der Quirin, so der Sommer" ("As St. Quirinus' Day goes, so will the summer").

Ice Saints is the name given to St. Mamertus, St. Pancras, and St. Servatus in German, Austrian, and Swiss folklore, so named because their feast days fall on the days of May 11, May 12, and May 13, respectively, a period noted to bring a brief spell of colder weather in the Northern Hemisphere under the Julian Calendar.

Iceland spar - Viking "sunstone"

*"the weather was thick and stormy . . . the king looked about and saw no blue sky .
. . then the king took the sunstone and held it up, and then he saw where [the Sun]
beamed from the stone."*
- *Hrafnas Saga*

"Bees do it. Ants do it. Did the Vikings do it? Can it be that the Vikings used the polarization of skylight as a navigation compass? Did the Vikings find their way to America by looking at the sky through a crystal, the proverbial sunstone?

The Icelandic sagas tell the story of how the Vikings sailed from Bergen on the coast of Norway to Iceland, continuing to Greenland and, likely, Newfoundland in the American continent. This remarkable sailing achievement was realized circa 700 -1100 CE, before the magnetic compass reached Europe from China (it wouldn't have helped much, anyway, so close to the Magnetic Pole). How did they steer true course in the long voyages out of land sight, especially in the common bad weather and low visibility of those high latitudes?

In 1967, a Danish archaeologist, Thorkild Ramskou, suggested that the Vikings might have used the polarization of the skylight for orientation when clouds hid the sun position. They would have used as polarizers natural crystals available to them, the famous sunstones described in the sagas. To find the location of the sun they only needed a clear patch of sky close to the zenith to determine the great circle passing through the sun. The pros and the cons of this theory are the following:

In favor:

1. In the Hrafnas Saga it says: "the weather was thick and stormy . . . The king looked about and saw no blue sky . . . then the king took the sunstone and held it up, and then he saw where [the Sun] beamed from the stone."

2. The crystal cordierite can be found as pebbles in the coast of Norway. It has birefringent and dichroic properties, changing color and brightness when rotated in front of polarized light. With an adequately cleaved crystal it is easy

to tell the direction of skylight polarization: its color will change (e.g. from blue to light yellow) when pointing towards the sun. [Curiously enough, the Vikings frequented Iceland, the first source of Iceland Spar (optical calcite), which has had such an important role in the discovery and study of polarization. Even today, many high-performance polarizers use that mineral]

3. At high latitude the sun remains for a long time close to the horizon, which produces the best skylight polarization pattern for navigation purposes.

4. Because of perspective, a bank of clouds of uniform density is squeezed together when looking far away. Thus, it is usually much easier to find a clear patch of sky towards the zenith (just try it). And crepuscular rays (the beams of light and darkness radiating from the sun when blocked by clouds) are difficult to see close to the zenith, as the line of sight crosses them through their thinnest section.

5. The method would have worked even when the sun was several degrees below the horizon (but still illuminating the atmosphere). Note that at twilight, when the sun is below the horizon by about two degrees, its location is very difficult to ascertain. Although a bright twilight arch can be seen, it occupies a large part of the horizon and is of uniform intensity. A similar effect may conceivably happen when the sun is above the horizon and a thick layer of clouds covers it.

6. Light fog and overcast of thin clouds don't eliminate skylight polarization.

Against:

1. Little detail is given to identify the sunstone and it is not mentioned specifically in relation to navigation or sailing.

2. The navigation season was, of course, summer when the sun is not that low during good part of the day nor is the weather very bad.

3. In all likelihood, the Viking sailor would have used a large number of clues from the sea and the sky to steer his ship. In many cases he could have interpolated the position of the sun between sightings or estimated its position. Many times it suffices to look at the pattern of illumination of the clouds, their iridescence, the direction of crepuscular rays or, close to twilight, the general illumination of the sky. Furthermore, the knowledge of the sun position is not sufficient for navigation. The helmsman needed to correct the sun direction for the time of the day and day of the year. Thus, he must have been quite a good reader of the sky and the sea.

4. Under a heavy overcast sky, when a navigational aid would be most useful, the polarization method doesn't work.

5. This theory is just a possibility, a statement of what the Vikings could have done, but it is based only in circumstantial evidence.

Interestingly, in the late 1940's the US National Bureau of Standards (now NIST) developed a Sky Compass based on the same principle. It was inspired by a previous "twilight compass" developed by Dr. A. H. Pfund of Johns Hopkins University. From a NBS 1949 paper: "The principal advantage of the sky compass . . . is during twilight, and when the sun is several degrees below the horizon, as well as when the region of the sky containing the sun is overcast, so long there is a clear patch of sky overhead. The sky compass is thus of particular value when the sun compass and the sextant are not usable. Since the extent of polarization of the sky's light is greatest at right angles to the incident beam of sunlight, the compass is most accurate in the polar regions, where it is also most useful, because of the long duration of twilight . . ." The US Navy and Air Force experimented with the sky compass in the 1950's and Scandinavian Airlines (SAS) used it for several years on its polar flights. Polarization.com has recently developed an inexpensive educational Skylight Compass Card.

When Ramskou originally proposed this theory, it was well received and widely accepted by the general public and also by the scientific community, and remained so for more than two decades. The Viking navigational triumphs became very fashionable, especially the exploits of Erik the Red and his son Leif (Ericksson) the "Lucky" circa 1000 AC, and the "discovery" of America centuries before Columbus. Both, Scientific American and National Geographic magazines carried the story of skylight navigation. However, in the 90's the theory was disputed on the basis that no real material proof exists and that the advantage provided to navigation would have been marginal. My personal take is that polarized skylight could have been of real use to the Vikings but, until direct evidence is found, one should be skeptic and stick to the simplest explanation: that the Norsemen where damn good sailors!"[16]

---

[16]By J. Alcoz

Figure 27 - Iceland Spar

"Whether the weather be fine, Whether the weather be not, Whether the weather be cold, Whether the weather be hot, We'll weather the weather, Whatever the whether, Whether we like it or not"
- Anon

Part 2
Body of the North

In **Part 2**, we'll explore the "body" of the north, studying the physical aspects of life. Essential to all balanced and integrated lifestyles are exercise, healing & rest, and food & drink.

I'll begin by introducing you to the simple, but highly beneficial practice of Runic Yoga - a short set of exercises you can do for life, and continue strengthening your connection to the runes and their power.

We'll next move on to Herblore, and modern uses; you'll be amazed at how long we've been using natural medicines, and how effective they are.

A satisfying end to every day must include good food and drink. In this regard we'll explore the mythic status of mead, and teach you how to make it. I've also included some interesting recipes from Anglo-Saxon England & Scandinavia.

Yoga teaches us to cure what need not be endured and endure what cannot be cured.
- B.K.S. Iyengar

Chapter 4 - Runic Yoga

unic Yoga or Stádhagaldr, is inspired by Yogic traditions stretching back thousands of years, and has combined the mysteries of the Runes - uniting two ancient and cherished traditions. The practice of Stádhagaldr looks very much like someone performing a simple Tai chi form; although I don't believe there to be any recent or direct connection between the two.

Yoga (Sanskrit) refers to traditional physical and mental disciplines originating in India. The word is associated with meditative practices in Hinduism, Buddhism, and Jainism. In Hinduism, it also refers to one of the six orthodox schools of Hindu philosophy, and to

28 - Cover of Marby's Runengymnastik from 1932

the goal toward which that school directs its practices. In Jainism it refers to the sum total of all activities—mental, verbal, and physical.

Inspired by the works of Guido von List in the 19'th century, the early 20th century German runemasters (F.B. Marby[17], S.A.

---

[17] Marby was imprisoned in the concentration camps by the Nazi's in WWII

Krummer, and Karl Spiesberger) developed runic yoga, or Runengymnastik, as a means of harnessing the streams of power present in the earth and atmosphere.

Following their development of Runengymnastik in the 1930's, there seems to be a gap of about fifty years with no mention of the practice. In 1984 Edred Thorsson (aka Stephen Flowers, Ph.D.) published his book *FUTHARK - A Handbook of Rune Magic*. In Thorsson's book, (pp. 124-132), he describes his discipline of stádhagaldr and its basis on Runengymnastik.

In parallel with the development of Runengymnastik and Stádhagaldr, evolved a holistic tradition in Norway, called Stav, which incorporated "Rune Stances" into its daily practice. The following section will discuss its history and evolution.

Modern Practices - Stav

The Hafskjold tradition of **Stav** is the only formal European Mind, Body & Spirit system that I am aware of. One of the core components of Stav is the practice of the Rune Stances based on the sixteen Runes of the Younger FUTHORC; Stav was my inspiration for further study into Stádhagaldr. Indeed, Stav has had a large influence on all aspects of this book, and although the Stádhagaldr I present here are based on the Elder FUTHARK, I embrace Stav and its principles and aims.

In 2005 I had the great honor and pleasure to have Graham Butcher, a Stav Master from Oxford, stay with our family and teach me the basics of Stav while he opened the American branch of his **Ice and Fire Stav** School. http://www.iceandfire.us/

During that time, I conducted an interview with him which outlines the Stav tradition.

Interview with a Stav Master

This interview was initially conducted in 2005, and updated in 2010.

Question: Graham, can you tell us what Stav is?

Graham Butcher: Sure, Stav is a European tradition of mind-body-spirit training; it literally means knowledge of the rune staves. That knowledge incorporates a philosophy of life and an underlying concept of how the universe works. A student should

29 - Graham Butcher

try to cultivate an awareness of how the universe works and aspire to integrate those principles into their way of life; Stav provides tools such as the runes, to help fulfill that aspiration.

Stav is really a path for individual enlightenment, which we call following one's own Wyrd (roughly – fate, destiny etc.).

It can help you:

* Develop awareness that there is a path(s);

* Inspire you to seek out a path, and

* Provide guidance, a framework, and tools to get on the path, but the tools Stav provides themselves are not THE path

Stav is more than a program of study, or a discipline, or a thing to follow or join, it's an opportunity to get to the underlying reality of the universe, – it's not like following the atkins diet, or joining amway.

Question: What are the tools & framework Stav provides?

Graham Butcher: Stav literally means "knowledge of the rune staves", so as you might imagine, Runes are a core tool in Stav. Stav uses the 16 runes of the younger futhork, meanings, and associations and knowledge.

The framework consists of:

30 - Graham demonstrating Fe

❄ Daily stances with the runes, that allow you to work with your body (somewhat resembles a simple Tai Chi form),

❄ 5 principles (Trell, Karl, Herse, Jarl, and Konge) which are really 5 key concepts of how to function as a human being, and

❄ Whatever other practices you choose to use, to live your life.

Good examples of additional practices are:

❄ Martial arts training, which provide a very good structure as it's testing the body, mind and spirit. It also explores the concepts of the lines of the web

❄ Working with health and well being, learning to understand how the body functions according to the web, and integrates with the natural energies and patterns of life, such as accessing the natural life energy of the universe.

❄ Understanding how society works and the webs and structures, observing this and analyzing social groups.

❄ Craft skills are another important aspect and use of natural materials such as leather, metal, cloth. We are learning to see how the web manifests itself in materials, and their use and application and construction of things. If something is made and works well, it's made in accordance with it's web. This actually carries on into all things, horticulture for example, and so on.

Question: Can you explain these 5 principles?

Graham Butcher: The 5 principles are based on the traditional Nordic class system, in mythology said to be introduced through the god Heimdall:

- Trel - Slave;
- Karl - Freeman;
- Herse (pronounced Hashyur) - Warrior;
- Jarl (pronounced Yarl) - Priest; and
- Konge (pronounced Kongyur) - King.

The 5 principles are metaphors for behaviors and reactions to life; For example, the **Trel** is responsible to, and dependent on others. He relies on others to tell him what to do, and neither wishes to, nor is expected to take responsibility or initiative.

The **Karl** or freeman is responsible for himself and his property. He confronts things only when they will affect him or his property and makes the best of it.

The **Herse** is responsible for the community. He moves in to confront things and takes control of them.

The **Jarl** is responsible for spiritual matters and healing and shifts reality so problems no longer affect him. The jarl deals with a much larger picture than the prior principles.

The **Konge** has mastered the other classes and uses whichever is most appropriate. He confronts things head on and uses their own weakness to take control.

This is a highly simplified version of the class system - it would be possible to write an entire book on the subject. Despite them being listed like this, the classes are actually cyclical, not linear: a Trel who realizes he has nothing to lose and turns this to his advantage has become a Konge; a Konge who worries if he's doing the right thing has become a Trel. Thus, to be a Trel is not a condemnation, rather it is a challenge to find one's own full potential.

Everyone has a natural affinity to one of the classes, which is discovered through a guided meditation. Once this is known, the practitioner can learn their own strengths and weaknesses and work with them according to their class. The classes are not a grading system or a measure of worth, but a way of seeing the Reality of one's own character. Within each class is a further division of the five classes - from Trel (ignoring one's class and trying to be what one is not) to Konge (in full control of one's class). It is up to the practitioner to achieve harmony within their class - ie, within their own nature.

Question: How long have you been practicing Stav, and do you have any other martial arts background?

Graham Butcher: I've been practicing Stav for 19 years and have the usual background in karate, kung-fu, kickboxing etc, when I was younger. I also have military training which I bring to my Stav training, which has a lot do to with socialization, and use of weapons etc.

Question: How did Stav come about?

Graham Butcher: The true origins are lost in time, but the core of the Stav tradition we have is passed down by the Hafskjold family of Norway who have lived in the same valley in Norway since around the 6'th century. The cores of the traditions such as the runes, basic stances, herb lore (traditionally the women's domain), boat building, bow making, training dogs, & horses – the skills that a warrior family needed down the ages. It was a traditional way of life.

No one knows the exact origin of the use of runes, but they have been shown through archeological sources to have a history of over 2000 years. In pagan Scandinavia the 16-stave futhark replaced the earlier 24-rune system at some point between the 6th and 9th centuries, this process beginning perhaps around the year 500.

According to the legends of the Hafskjold family, Stav as we know it dates from circa the year 500 and has been practiced by the family since this time. Oral history naturally cannot be tested in the same way as an archaeological or textual record, but there is no evidence to suggest the family's legends are inaccurate.

31- Ivar Hafskjold

As far as weapons go, the staff was the basic tool as it was used as a walking staff, ski poll, short spear etc. The Hafskjolds developed this for fighting and passed this down through the family.

Ivar's grandfather demonstrated to him, five concepts with the staff that related to the five principles in Stav. By the time that Ivar was really interested in learning, his uncles and grandfather were too old to give him the intense training he wanted, so he looked elsewhere to help flesh out his training. He realized in his early thirties that he wanted to learn how to do the traditional martial arts properly, and he wanted to ensure the continuity of his family traditions and find ways of improving them via other sources. So he went to Japan in order to learn traditional Japanese martial arts. He had seen the book on the Jo before he went, and thought this would be a good starting point.

After this Ivar found his way to Jo-do, and did some Iaido, but was really looking for Jo-Jitsu (jutsu). While in his jodo grading, Ivar met a gentlemen that taught Jo-jitsu and ken-jitsu; after which, this became his focus and eventually achieved 4'th dan in both of these arts – which is very impressive for a westerner. After 14 years of training and teaching, Ivar decide to come back to Europe and settled in England.

He made himself available to teach; there was an article in fighting arts international where Ivar was profiled and covered his Japanese experience and his family tradition. I was teaching elsewhere at the time and after reading this article, I tracked down Ivar and asked to train with him.

The bottom line is that this system has not come down unchanged for 1500 years, which some people seem confused about, and which causes unnecessary controversy. The core concepts of the web, stances, runes etc. are what were passed down.

Some things have been lost, Ivar has added new material, and has revived others – like some of the weapons that were used in old times. He has done this by synthesizing his Japanese martial arts experience and the components of Stav that were passed down to him. The result of which is a holistic system, rooted history that has been able to benefit from other systems and has evolved over time organically - as all living things do, and should.

Question: How has Stav evolved, what has changed?

Graham Butcher: David Watkinson and I became Ivar's first students in England. David then went on to create a highly developed unarmed system, based on Stav. I started integrating Stav into martial arts classes I was already teaching and gradually began developing a training system in parallel with Ivar, then after a couple of years started advertising more widely. During this time, an International network was being built.

We started using the staff principally and also the Japanese weapons (jo & boken) and techniques to explore them for the first couple of years after Ivar came back from Japan. Soon, I started looking at using more traditional European weapons, making the system more tailored to our region, and bringing back some of the Historic tools such as longer staves, battle-axe etc., all of which became the basis for my own training.

32 - Battle-Axe Training

Ivar then developed some drills using the longer staff and battle-axe which I used for my own training, and that of my students. Later, Ivar started working with the long sword, and started cutting and adapting to the 5 principles, and seeing the lines.

After about 4 years of working with Ivar, I moved down to Oxford, and started teaching independently and building up a student base. There we continued to develop the training, and tailored some exercises to create a foundational staff training curriculum, which is more relevant to modern students with a sedentary lifestyle – we needed to get them moving and develop them at a low level, then they could progress to more advanced and demanding techniques.

In recent years I've been ensuring that there is a teachable system, so that the system is consistent if you work with one of my authorized teachers, and I've also been exploring the health and social implications.

Question: What does a typical Stav Training Session entail?

Graham Butcher: Classes will usually begin and end with a group practice of the rune stances. Then we follow the stances with the basic staff exercises which relate to one of the runes stances and incorporate breathing, strength, coordination and skill, balance and body awareness.

Most session would then also include some practice of the 5 two person drill practiced with that staff through which the student can learn to work with the 5 principles of Stav.

From then on, the classes may cover a wide range of martial skills such as working with the battle-axe, spear, 2-handed long sword, sax (1 handed single edge knife / short sword), and cudgel. Which makes 6 traditional weapons (including the staff). There are three more, less commonly used weapons, which are: the longbow, throwing-hammer, and tein (very short stick, similar to a kubotan).

There are basically three things we do with the weapons:

- ❋ Cutting or striking drills
- ❋ Drills to explore the 5 principles
- ❋ Working with 9 guard positions

We also explore self-defense via the tein & unarmed technique.

Question: How can someone learn more about Stav, or visit a class?

Graham Butcher: We have schools in the UK and the USA, so please visit us at **www.iceandfire.org.uk** for more details.

Runic Yoga or "Stádhagaldr"

The physical portions of the Stádhagaldr presented below rely heavily on my Stav experience, while the esoteric nature and foundation is derived from the Elder Futhark and the works of Edred Thorsson et al.

My intent is to present a practice that is easily accessible, and captures the nature of the Elder Futhark.

Goals & Benefits of Stádhagaldr

Per (Thorsson, A Handbook of Rune Magic, 1984) "The overall aims of the stádhagaldr are:

1. Control of the body through posture (stadha)

2. Control of thought through song (galdr)

3. Control of breath

4. Control of emotion

5. Becoming aware of the rune realms of the self and the world(s)

6. Control and direction of the will."

"...Stádhagaldr is used as a mode of psychological integration and personal transmutation…"

Another benefit of performing the runic postures is the strengthening of your relationship with, and understanding of the Runes. By practicing their forms daily, and allowing each of their meanings to wash over you, you should develop a deep understanding of their relevance and applications in your own life.

The regular practice of Stádhagaldr can also illuminate other aspects of your life; as you're practicing the postures, perhaps you make a mistake. Why is this? What else is going on that is affecting you? How are you feeling? What are your body and your connection with the rest of the multiverse telling you?

I remember hearing people talk about the "runners high", that sense of elation you feel during a long distance run. Although stádhagaldr isn't nearly as rigorous physically, there are times when I do get that sense of elation, contentment, and reflection – perhaps it's the mind or spirit undergoing that rigorous activity. Yiannis Kouros, who is a legend in the world of Ultrarunning responded to a question about what he felt when he ran.

"Some may ask why I am running such long distances. There are reasons. During the ultras I come to a point where my body is almost dead. My mind has to take leadership. When it is very hard there is a war going on between the body and the mind. If my body wins, I will have to give up; if my mind wins, I will continue. At that time I feel that I stay outside of my body. It is as if I see my body in front of me; my mind commands and my body follows. This is a very special feeling, which I like very much. . . It is a very beautiful feeling and the only time I experience my personality separate from my body, as two different things."

I would posit that perhaps it isn't a **separation** of personality and body Yiannis is feeling, but **Integration**; his mind and body have finally stopped fighting for control, and have given in to their synergistic power. Although I don't expect I will reach some persistent state of Nirvana, the glimpses I get through my exercises and mediation are amazing, and I cherish each experience.

Getting Started

Typically we perform two full sets of the runic postures (one set represents 24 runes), and if possible perform the first set in the morning and the second set in the evening. The intent is to welcome the sun (Sunna) as she rises, and bid her goodnight.

Another tradition is that we pay respect to the North, the home of our ancestors and spiritual inspiration for the stádhagaldr; as such, we imagine that our postures are being viewed from the North.

The first set is performed facing east, and as we imagine that they are being viewed from the North they appear as mirror images. When we conduct the second set facing west, the runes will be oriented as we normally see them.

The postures can be done with or without the galdr (chanting the rune name or sound). I recommend you start doing it without galdr until you are comfortable with all the mechanics and sequences of the runes. Once you are comfortable with the basics, feel free to add galdr, and perhaps even create your own combinations for specific meditations.

General Guidance

- Consult a Physician before performing any new exercise
- Find a quiet place, free from distractions to perform your stádhagaldr
- Outside in nature is preferred – try a park, or even your backyard
- Wear loose and comfortable clothing if possible
- Can be done with Galdr (chanting the rune name), or without
- Postures can be done one or a few at a time, to focus on certain aspects of the runes for meditative purposes or spell work
- Feel the meaning of each Rune as you take on its form, consider it's associations

First Set

Both sets start facing North in the Ready Posture. In the first set, after the **Nine Breaths** and **Hailing the North**, you turn <u>East</u> in order to greet the Sun as she rises, and begin your postures. Don't worry if you're doing them later in the day - it's a symbolic gesture.

The first set of stances focus on the **Left side of your body**

Relax

Stand facing North, relaxed, with your arms at your side, and release all tension in your shoulders. Take a minute to relax your mind, and dispel any lingering thoughts. Have your knees very slightly bent, and tense your buttocks a little to align your spine.

9 Breaths

When you feel you are ready to begin, start your nine breaths. Breathe in naturally, and exhale by flexing your stomach. Focus on breathing out.

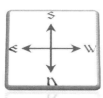

NOTE: All pictures of the stances appear as if viewed by another person who has their back to the North, and are looking South.

For convenience I have added a small compass graphic to the left of each image.

The compass appears reversed, as it is showing the orientation of the model performing the stances – in the picture to the right, Leigh is facing North

Figure 33 - Ready Posture
Demonstrated by my model Leigh

Hail the North

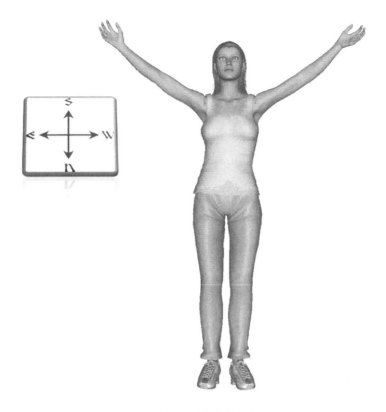

Figure 34 - Hail the North

- When you have finished your nine breaths, look up, with arms upraised, and hail the North - the symbolic home of our ancestors.
- Remember those who came before.
- You are Facing North.

1 - Fehu – Livestock, Wealth, Energy, Fertility, Creation

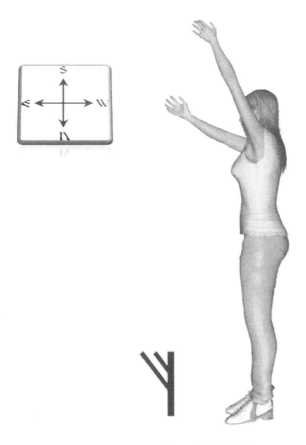

Figure 35 - Fehu Posture

- ▲ Look to your right, and then slowly turn to the right, sweeping your right foot out. You will now be facing east.
- ▲ Inhale as you slowly raise your arms so that your left arm is slightly above your right arm as shown above. Hold it there for about 2 seconds, then slowly lower your arms and return to the ready position - gently exhaling as you do
- ▲ If you're meditating on the Runes, think about some of the associations and keywords listed above as you perform the posture.

2 - Uruz – The Aurochs, Health, Wisdom, Vital Strength

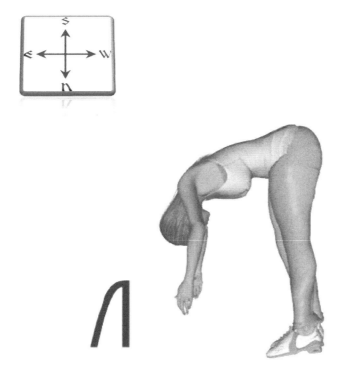

Figure 36 - Uruz Posture

⚑ Inhale fully before you bend over, hold it, then bend over at the hips to form the posture as shown – ensure the muscles in your upper body are relaxed. Hold the posture for a second or two.

⚑ Exhale as you straighten up, and gently return to the ready position.

3 - Thurisaz – Giant, Thorn, Destruction/ Defense

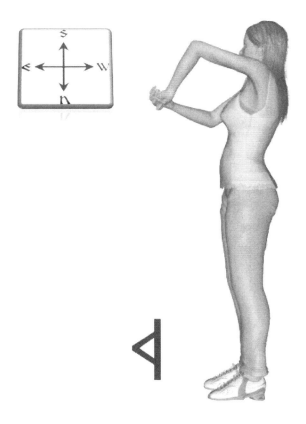

Figure 37 - Thurisaz Posture

🔺 Make a fist with your left hand, and place it in the palm of your right hand. Then as you inhale, gently push your arms out in front of you as shown.

🔺 Relax and return to the ready position as you exhale.

4 - Ansuz – god (Odinn), Mouth, Song, Poetry, Inspiration, Knowledge

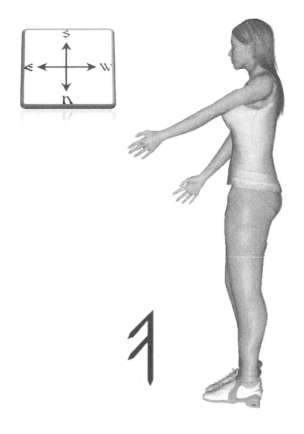

Figure 38 - Ansuz Posture

🔺 Inhale as you slowly raise your arms so that your left arm is slightly above your right arm as shown. Hold it there for about 2 seconds, then slowly lower your arms and return to the ready posture - gently exhaling as you do.

87

5 - Raido – Ride, Journey, a Path, Ritual, Rhythm

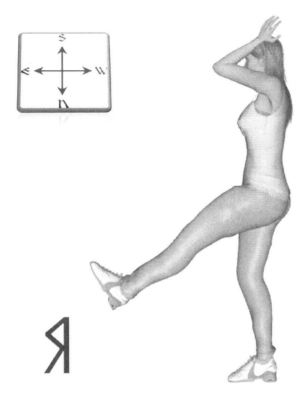

Figure 39 - Raido Posture

- Begin this posture by bending the right knee a little bit more, and shifting your weight to the right leg prior to lifting your left leg – this will help you keep your balance.
- Raise your left leg and arm slowly as you inhale, trying to finish their movements at the same time.
- Relax and return to the ready position as you exhale, again trying to synchronize when the arm and leg have returned to their neutral positions.

6 - Kenaz – Torch, Enlightenment, Hearth, Controlled Energy, Creativity

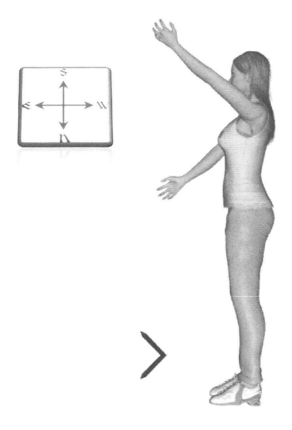

Figure 40 - Kenaz Posture

🔺 Inhale as you slowly raise your arms so that your left arm is much higher than your right arm as shown. Hold it there for about 2 seconds, then slowly lower your arms and return to the ready posture - gently exhaling as you do.

89

7 - Gebo – Gift, sacrifice, hospitality

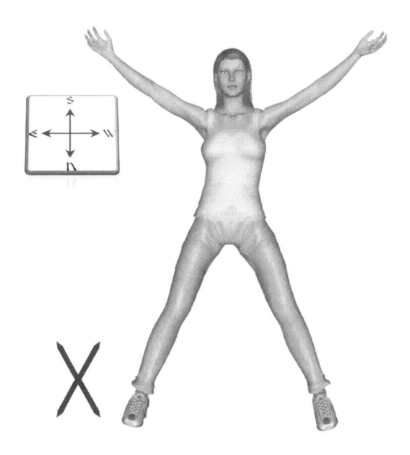

Figure 41 - Gebo Posture

- Look to your left, and then slowly turn to the left, sweeping your left foot out. You will now be facing north.
- Inhale as you raise your arms as shown. Hold it there for about 2 seconds, then slowly lower your arms and return to the ready posture - gently exhaling as you do. Your left leg will come back in.

8 - Wunjo – Joy, hope, Well Being, Binding, Fellowship

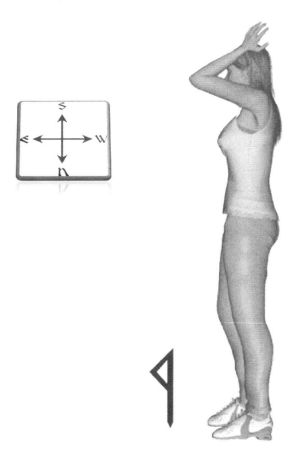

Figure 42 - Wunjo Posture

- Look to your right, and then slowly turn to the right, sweeping your right foot out. You will now be facing east once again.
- Inhale as you raise your left arm as shown. Your right arm will remain at your side. Hold it there for about 2 seconds, then slowly lower your arm and return to the ready posture - gently exhaling as you do.

9a - Hagalaz – Hail, Transformation, Evolution, Destruction, Seed of Primal Life

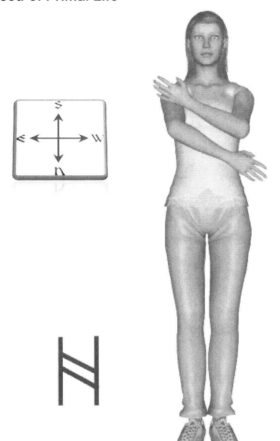

> **There are 2 forms of the Hagalaz runestave:**
>
> The first *appears as you see on this page which resembles the Latin letter* **H**, *and is found in the* Elder Futhark

Figure 43 - Hagalaz Static Posture

- ♠ Look to your left, and then slowly turn to the left, sweeping your left foot out. You will now be facing north.
- ♠ Inhale as you cross your arms across your chest as shown
- ♠ Hold it there for about 2 seconds, then slowly lower your arms and return to the ready posture - gently exhaling as you do.

9b - Hagalaz – Hail, Transformation, Evolution, Destruction, Seed of Primal Life

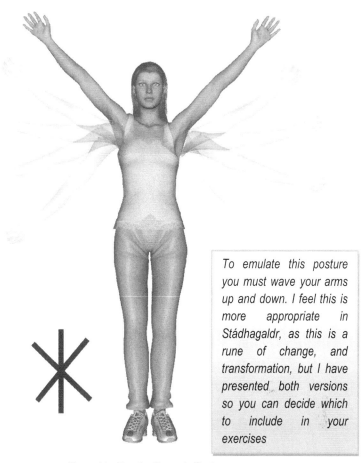

To emulate this posture you must wave your arms up and down. I feel this is more appropriate in Stádhagaldr, as this is a rune of change, and transformation, but I have presented both versions so you can decide which to include in your exercises

Figure 44 - Hagalaz Dynamic Posture

- The **second** form of Hagalaz, found in the Younger Futhorc, appears more like a grain of hail, which it represents.
- In this alternate form of the Hagalaz posture, you will start by raising your arms up as in the "Hail the North" posture, then place them down at your side, back up and down 2 more times - For a total of 3 complete motions up and down. Take care not to wave your arms too forcefully, this is a gentle exercise.
- Breath naturally as you performs this posture.

10 - Nauthiz – Need, Deliverance from Distress, Resistance

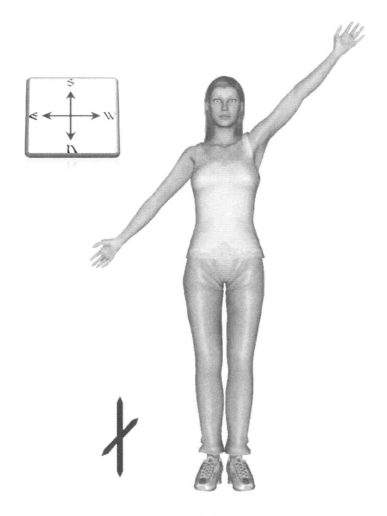

Figure 45 - Nauthiz Posture

- ♠ Inhale as you raise your arms – left high, and right low, as shown
- ♠ Hold it there for about 2 seconds, then slowly lower your arms and return to the ready posture - gently exhaling as you do.

11 - Isa – Ice, Preservation, Lack of Motion, Ego, Anti-Matter, Concentration

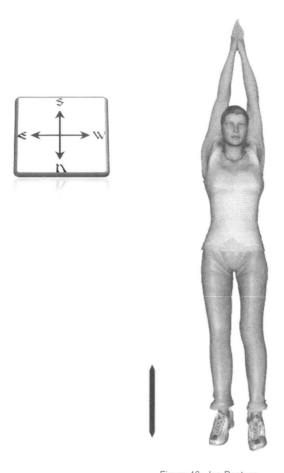

Figure 46 - Isa Posture

🔺 Inhale as you place your palms together and stretch your arms above your head, and be on the tips of your toes – try to stretch as far as possible.

🔺 Hold it for about 2 seconds, then slowly lower your arms and return to the ready posture - gently exhaling as you do.

12 - Jera – Year, Harvest, Reward, Fruition

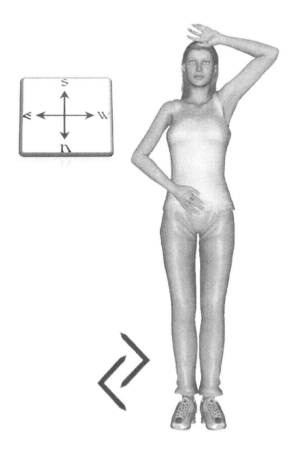

Figure 47 - Jera Posture

- Inhale as you raise your arms – left high, and right low, as shown
- Hold it there for about 2 seconds, then slowly lower your arms and return to the ready posture - gently exhaling as you do.

13 - Eihwaz – Yew, World Tree, Vertical Cosmic Axis, Life / Death, Protection, Endurance

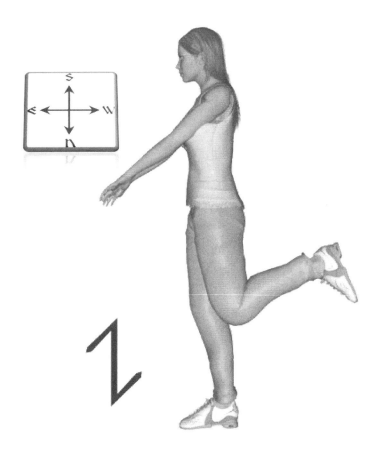

Figure 48 - Eiwhaz Posture

- Look to your right, and then slowly turn to the right, sweeping your right foot out. You will now be facing east once again.
- As in the Raido posture, bend your right knee slightly and shift your weight to the left prior to lifting your left leg off the ground – this will aid in balance.
- Raise both arms around waist height as shown – time the lifting of the left leg to finish as your hands do.
- Hold it there for about 2 seconds, then slowly lower your arms and left leg, and return to the ready posture - gently exhaling as you do.

14 - Pertho – Dice Cup, Chance, Birth, Wyrd, Orlog, The Nouns, Time

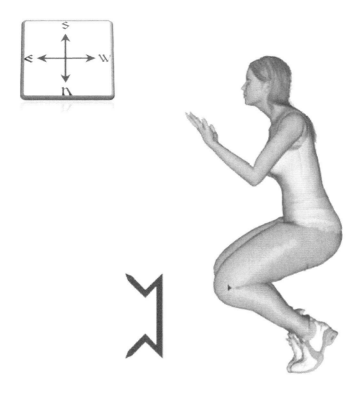

Figure 49 - Pertho Posture

🔺 Inhale as you pull your elbows in together and have your forearms meet, palms up. Try to keep your elbows as close to your body as possible.

🔺 As you pull in your arms, crouch on the tips of your toes, and bend your legs at about 45 degrees -   as shown above

🔺 Hold it there for about 2 seconds, then slowly lower your arms and return to the ready posture - gently exhaling as you do.

15 – Algiz – Elk, Protection, Sanctuary, Life, Bifrost, Connection between gods and men

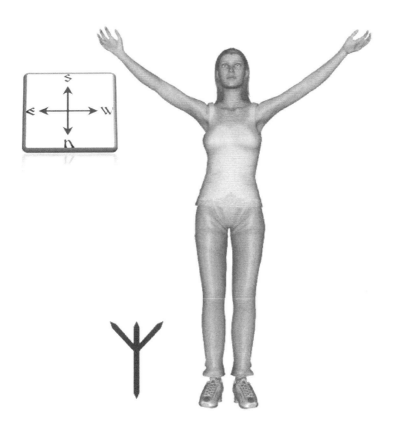

Figure 50 - Algiz Posture

🔺 Algiz is fairly simple, and looks exactly like the "Hail the North" posture.

🔺 Look to your left, and then slowly turn to the left, sweeping your left foot out. You will now be facing north.

🔺 Inhale as you raise your arms upward.

🔺 Hold it there for about 2 seconds, then slowly lower your arms and return to the ready posture - gently exhaling as you do.

16 – Sowilo – Sun, Guide, Goal and Path, Success, Honor

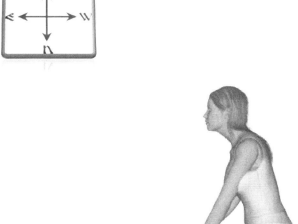

Figure 51 - Sowilo Posture

- Look to your right, and then slowly turn to the right, sweeping your right foot out. You will now be facing east once again.
- Inhale as you place your palms on your thighs, and crouch on your toes, with your calves meeting the backs of your legs
- Hold it there for about 2 seconds, and then slowly return to the ready posture - gently exhaling as you do.

17 - Teiwhaz – The god Tyr, Law, Justice, Victory, Self-Sacrifice, Spiritual Discipline

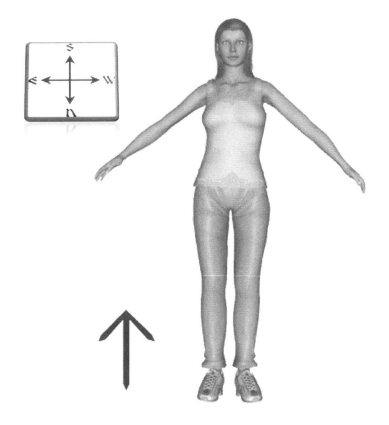

Figure 52 - Teiwhaz Posture

▲ Look to your left, and then slowly turn to the left, sweeping your left foot out. You will now be facing north.

▲ Inhale as you raise your arms upward slightly.

▲ Hold it there for about 2 seconds, then slowly lower your arms and return to the ready posture - gently exhaling as you do.

18 – Berkana – Birch, Earth Mother, Renewal, Birth-Life-Death Cycle

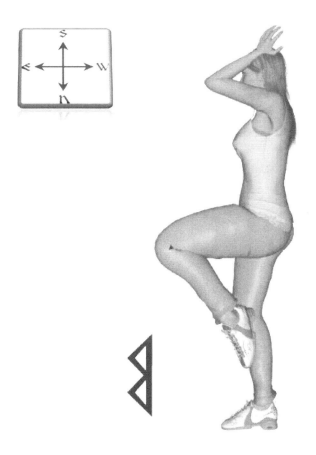

Figure 53 - Berkana Posture

- ⚜ Look to your right, and then slowly turn to the right, sweeping your right foot out. You will now be facing East once again.
- ⚜ As in the Raido posture, bend your right knee slightly and shift your weight to the left prior to lifting your left leg off the ground to aid in balance.
- ⚜ Raise your right arm as shown, placing the palm near your temple.
- ⚜ While raising your arm, lift your left leg, placing your foot on the right knee
- ⚜ Hold it there for about 2 seconds, then slowly lower your left leg and arm, and return to the ready posture - gently exhaling as you do.

19 – Ehwaz – Horse, Fertility, Vehicle for Otherworldly Journeys, Trust, Loyalty, Legal Marriage

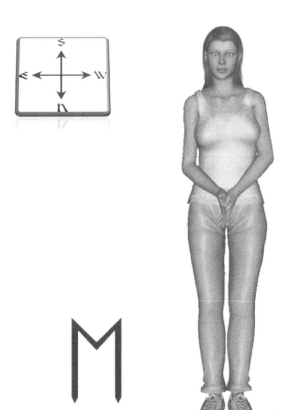

Figure 54 - Ehwaz Posture

- 🔺 Look to your left, and then slowly turn to the left, sweeping your left foot out. You will now be facing North.
- 🔺 Gently place your palms together and place them just under your naval
- 🔺 Hold it there for about 2 seconds, and return to the ready posture - gently exhaling as you do.

20 – Mannaz – Human, Intelligence, Divine Structure, Self-Realization, Fulfillment

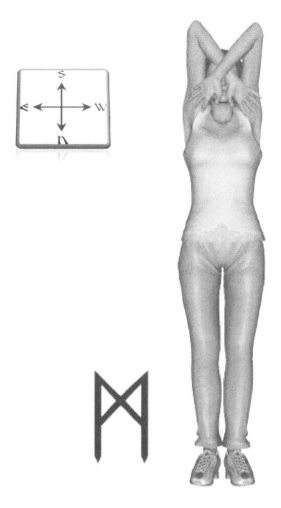

Figure 55 - Mannaz Posture

▲ Inhale as you raise both arms as shown, left over right – elbows should be as high as possible.

▲ Hold it there for about 2 seconds, and return to the ready posture - gently exhaling as you do.

21 – Laguz – Water, Life, Growth, Flow, Basic Energy, Source of Life

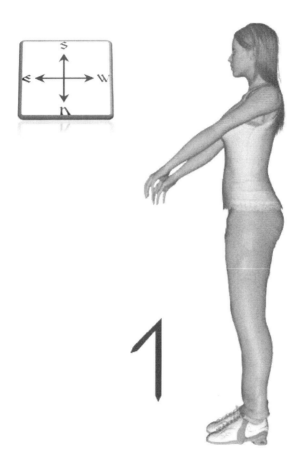

Figure 56 - Laguz Posture

▲ Look to your right, and then slowly turn to the right, sweeping your right foot out. You will now be facing East once again.

▲ Inhale as you slowly raise both arms about waist height as shown

▲ Hold it there for about 2 seconds, and return to the ready posture - gently exhaling as you do.

22 – Inguz – The God Ingvi Frey, Potential Energy, Gestation, Seed

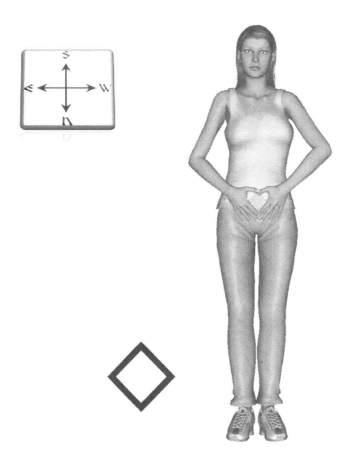

Figure 57 - Inguz Posture

- ⚑ Look to your left, and then slowly turn to the left, sweeping your left foot out. You will now be facing north.
- ⚑ Inhale as you place both hands together – thumb to thumb, index finger to index finger and hold them just under your naval.
- ⚑ Hold it there for about 2 seconds, and return to the ready posture - gently exhaling as you do.

23 – Dagaz – Day, Light, Polarity, A Turning Point

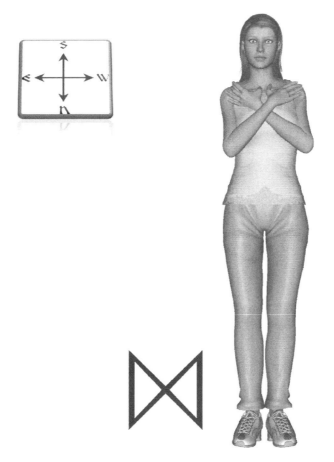

Figure 58 - Dagaz Posture

🔺 Inhale as you cross your arms over your chest, left over right as shown.
🔺 Hold it there for about 2 seconds, and return to the ready posture - gently exhaling as you do.

24 – Othala – Property, Inheritance, Sacred Enclosure

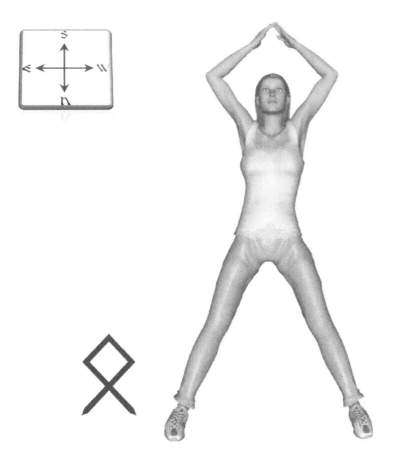

Figure 59 - Othala Posture

⚠ Inhale as you step out with your left foot, and raise both arms up as shown – finger tip to finger tip

⚠ Hold it there for about 2 seconds, and return to the ready posture - gently exhaling as you do.

Second Set

The second set will be performed facing West, and once again the runes will be represented as viewed from the North, but in this case will now be oriented as we normally see them.

The second set will focus on the **Right side of the body.**

I won't included a detailed description of each posture for the second set, as they are simply a reverse of the first set; if you raised your left arm high in Fehu for the first set, you will raise your right arm high for the second set and so on.

At the end of the first set, you should be facing North. If you are doing the sets back to back, you will simply turn to the West and begin. Once all 24 postures are complete, we conclude with 9 breaths, as we started the first set.

If you are performing your second some time after the first, don't forget to take a minute to relax and get your mind ready.

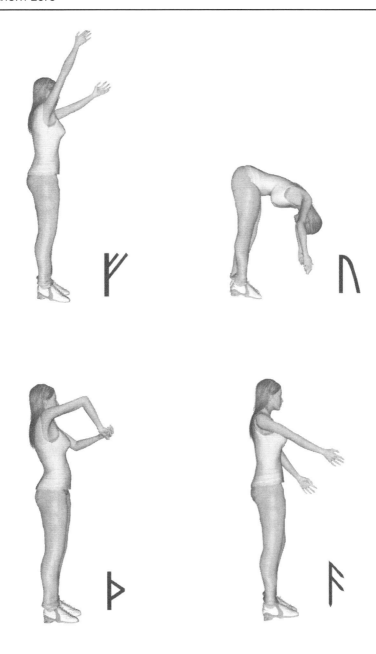

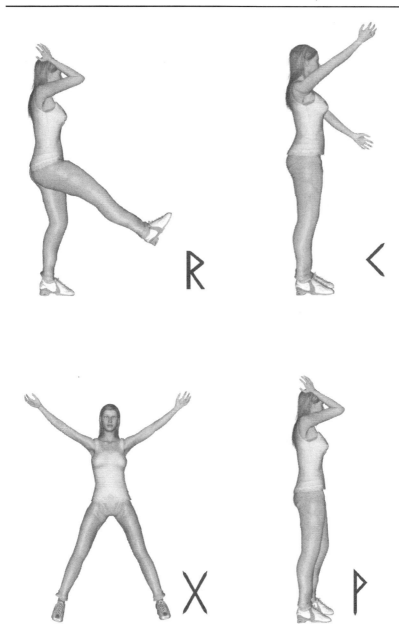

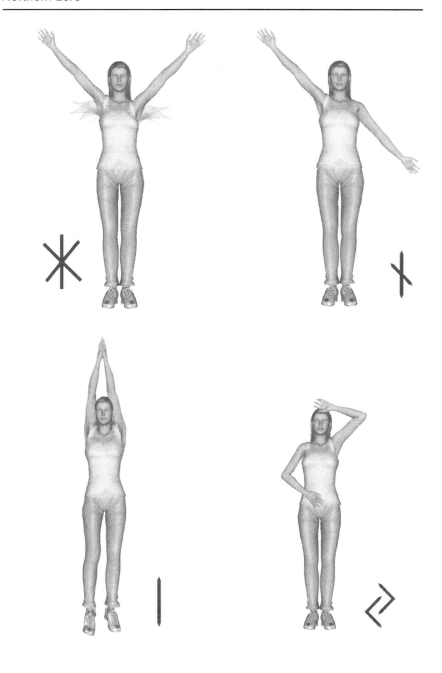

112

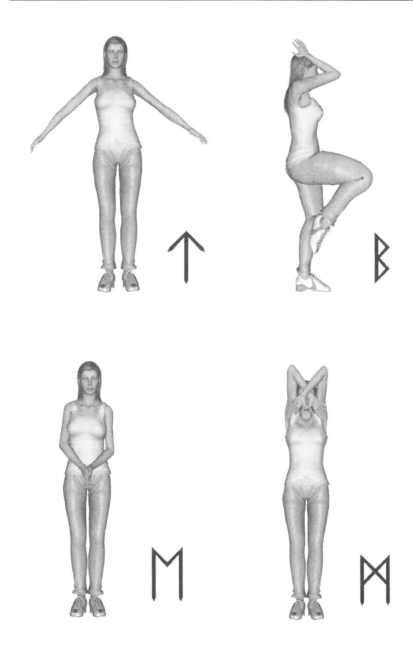

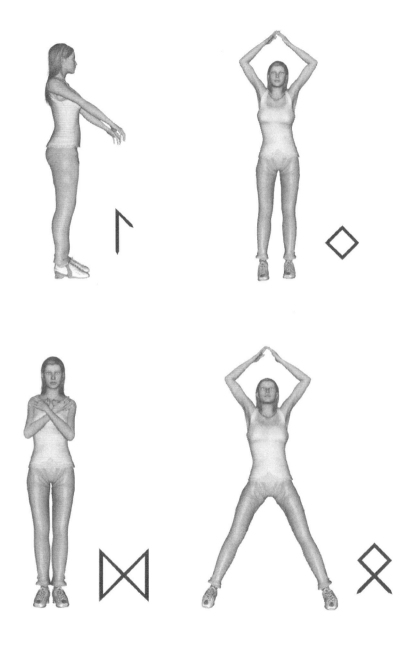

Once you have completed the second set, return to the ready position, and take 9 breaths as at the start of the first set.

Hail the North to finish. You have now finished two full sets of stádhagaldr!

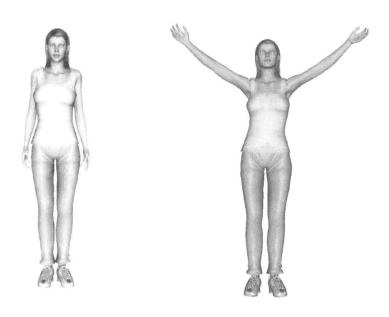

Further Work

As we mentioned before, once you feel comfortable with the basic stances, you might want to start adding the galdr, creating your own combinations for particular meditative exercises etc.

I will be following up with a book on advanced Stádhagaldr, but until then, Stádhagaldr is yours to explore!

Chapter 5 - Herb Lore & Leechcraft

ature, in the broadest sense, is equivalent to the natural world, physical world, or material world. "Nature" refers to the phenomena of the physical world, and also to life in general. It ranges in scale from the subatomic to the cosmic. The term "nature" may refer to living plants and animals, geological processes, weather, and physics, such as matter and energy. The term is often refers to the "natural environment" or wilderness - wild animals, rocks, forest, beaches, and in general areas that have not been substantially altered by humans, or which persist despite human intervention. For, example, manufactured objects and human interaction are generally not considered part of nature, unless qualified as, for example, "human nature" or "the whole of nature". This more traditional concept of "nature" implies a distinction between natural and artificial elements of the Earth, with the artificial as that which has been brought into being by a human consciousness or a human mind.

In this chapter, we'll explore a sampling of the Herb Lore at our disposal and find out what plants and animal products our ancestors relied on for health and well being.

Herb Lore, or Herbalism, is a traditional medicinal or folk medicine practice based on the use of plants and plant extracts. Herbalism is also known as botanical medicine, medical herbalism, herbal medicine, herbology, and phytotherapy. The scope of herbal medicine is sometimes extended to include fungal and bee products, as well as minerals, shells and certain animal parts.

People on all continents have used hundreds to thousands of indigenous plants for treatment of ailments since prehistoric times. Medicinal herbs were found in the personal effects of an "ice man", whose body was frozen in the Swiss Alps for more than 5,300 years. These herbs appear to have been used to treat the parasites found in his intestines. Anthropology or anthropologists theorize that animals evolved a tendency to seek out bitter plant parts in response to illness.

Indigenous healers often claim to have learned by observing that sick animals change their food preferences to nibble at bitter herbs they would normally reject. Field biologists have provided corroborating evidence based on observation of diverse species, such as chimpanzees, chickens, sheep and butterflies. Lowland gorillas take 90% of their diet from the fruits of *Aframomum melegueta*, a relative of the ginger plant, that is a potent antimicrobial and apparently keeps shigellosis and similar infections at bay.

The use of herbs and spices in cuisine developed in part as a response to the threat of food-borne pathogens. Studies show that in tropical climates where pathogens are the most abundant, recipes are the most highly spiced. Further, the spices with the most potent antimicrobial activity tend to be selected. In all cultures vegetables are spiced less than meat, presumably because they are more resistant to spoilage.

Herbs in history

In the written record, the study of herbs dates back over 5,000 years to the Sumerians, who described well-established medicinal uses for such plants as laurel, caraway, and thyme. Ancient Egyptian medicine of 1000 B.C. are known to have used garlic, opium, castor oil, coriander, mint, indigo, and other herbs for medicine and the Old Testament also mentions herb use and cultivation, including mandrake, vetch, caraway, wheat, barley, and rye.

Indian **Ayurveda** medicine has used herbs such as turmeric possibly as early as 1900 BCE. Many other herbs and minerals used in Ayurveda were later described by ancient Indian herbalists such as Charaka and Sushruta during the 1st millenium BCE. The *Sushruta Samhita* attributed to Sushruta in the 6th century BCE describes 700 medicinal plants, 64 preparations from mineral sources, and 57 preparations based on animal sources.

The first Chinese herbal book, the *Shennong Bencao Jing*, compiled during the Han Dynasty but dating back to a much earlier date, possibly 2700 B.C., lists 365 medicinal plants and their uses - including ma-Huang, the shrub that introduced the drug ephedrine to modern medicine. Succeeding generations augmented on the *Shennong Bencao Jing*, as in the *Yaoxing Lun (Treatise on the Nature of Medicinal Herbs)*, a 7th century Tang Dynasty treatise on herbal medicine.

The ancient Greeks and Romans made medicinal use of plants and their medicinal practices, as preserved in the writings of Hippocrates and - especially - Galen, provided the pattern for later western medicine. Hippocrates advocated the use of a few simple herbal drugs - along with fresh air, rest, and proper diet. Galen, on the other hand, recommended large doses of drug mixtures - including plant, animal, and mineral ingredients. The Greek physician compiled the first European treatise on the properties and uses of medicinal plants, *De Materia Medica*. In the first century CE, Dioscorides wrote a compendium of more than 500 plants that remained an authoritative reference into the 17th century. Similarly important for herbalists and botanists of later centuries was the Greek book that founded the science of botany, Theophrastus' *Historia Plantarum*, written in the fourth century BCE

The uses of plants for medicine and other purposes changed little in early medieval Europe. Many Greek and Roman writings on medicine, as on other subjects, were preserved by hand copying of manuscripts in monasteries. The monasteries thus tended to become local centers of medical knowledge, and their herb gardens provided the raw materials for simple treatment of common disorders. At the same time, folk medicine in the home and village continues uninterrupted, supporting numerous wandering and settled herbalists. Among these were the "wise-women," who prescribed herbal remedies often along with spells and enchantments. It was not until the late Middle Ages that women who were knowledgeable in herb lore became the targets of the witch hysteria. One of the most famous women in the herbal tradition was Hildegard of Bingen. A twelfth century Benedictine nun, she wrote a medical text called *Causes and Cures*.

Medical schools known as Bimaristan began to appear from the 9th century in the medieval Islamic world, which was generally more advanced than medieval Europe at the time. The Arabs venerated Greco-Roman culture and learning, and translated tens of thousands of texts into Arabic for further study. As a trading culture, the Arab travellers had access to plant material from distant places such as China and India. Herbals, medical texts and translations of the classics of antiquity filtered in from east and west. Muslim botanists and Muslim physicians significantly expanded on the earlier knowledge of materia medica. For example, al-Dinawari described more than 637 plant drugs in the 9th century, and Ibn al-Baitar described more than 1,400 different plants, foods and drugs, over 300 of which were his own original discoveries, in the 13th century. The experimental scientific method was introduced into the field of materia medica in the 13th century by the Andalusian-Arab botanist Abu al-Abbas al-Nabati, the teacher of Ibn al-Baitar. Al-Nabati introduced empirical techniques in the testing, description and identification of numerous materia medica, and he separated unverified reports from those supported by actual tests and observations. This allowed the study of materia medica to evolve into the science of pharmacology.

Avicenna's *The Canon of Medicine* (1025) is considered the first pharmacopoeia, and lists 800 tested drugs, plants and minerals. Book Two (of 14 volumes) is devoted to a discussion of the healing properties of herbs, including nutmeg, senna, sandalwood, rhubarb, myrrh, cinnamon, and rosewater. Baghdad was an important center for Arab herbalism, as was Al-Andalus between 800 and 1400. Abulcasis (936-1013) of Cordoba authored The Book of Simples, an important source for later European herbals, while Ibn al-Baitar (1197–1248) of Malaga authored the Corpus of Simples, the most complete Arab herbal which introduced 200 new healing herbs, including tamarind, aconite, and nux vomica. Other pharmacopoeia books include that written by Abu-Rayhan Biruni in the 11th century and Ibn Zuhr (Avenzoar) in the 12th century (and printed in 1491), The origins of clinical pharmacology also date back to the Middle Ages in Avicenna's The Canon of Medicine, Peter of Spain's Commentary on Isaac, and John of St Amand's Commentary on the Antedotary of Nicholas. In particular, the Canon introduced clinical trials, randomized controlled trials, and efficacy tests.

The second millennium saw the beginning of a slow erosion of the pre-eminent position held by plants as sources of therapeutic effects. This began with the Black Death, which the then dominant *Four Element* medical system proved powerless to stop. A century later, Paracelsus introduced the use of active chemical drugs (like arsenic, copper sulfate, iron, mercury, and sulfur). These were accepted even though they had toxic effects because of the urgent need to treat Syphilis. The rapid development of chemistry and the other physical sciences, led increasingly to the dominance of chemotherapy - chemical medicine - as the orthodox system of the twentieth century.

Herbalism Today

The use of herbs to treat disease is almost universal among non-industrialized societies. A number of traditions came to dominate the practice of herbal medicine at the end of the twentieth century:

- The "classical" herbal medicine system, based on Greek and Roman sources

- The Siddha and Ayurvedic medicine systems from various South Asian Countries

- Chinese herbal medicine (Chinese herbology)

- Unani-Tibb medicine

- Shamanic herbalism: a catch-all phrase for information mostly supplied from South America and the Himalayas

Many of the pharmaceuticals currently available to physicians have a long history of use as herbal remedies, including opium, aspirin, digitalis, and quinine. The World Health Organization (WHO) estimates that 80 percent of the world's population presently uses herbal medicine for some aspect of primary health care. Pharmaceuticals are prohibitively expensive for most of the world's population, half of which lives on less than $2 U.S. per day. In comparison, herbal medicines can be grown from seed or gathered from nature for little or no cost. Herbal medicine is a major component in all traditional medicine systems, and a common element in Siddha, Ayurvedic, homeopathic, naturopathic, traditional Chinese medicine, and Native American medicine.

The use of, and search for, drugs and dietary supplements derived from plants have accelerated in recent years. Pharmacologists, microbiologists, botanists, and natural-products chemists are combing the Earth for phytochemicals and leads that could be developed for treatment of various diseases. In fact, according to the World Health Organisation, approximately 25% of modern drugs used in the United States have been derived from plants. Three quarters of plants that provide active ingredients for prescription drugs came to the attention of researchers because of their use in traditional medicine.

Among the 120 active compounds currently isolated from the higher plants and widely used in modern medicine today, 80 percent show a positive correlation between their modern therapeutic use and the traditional use of the plants from which they are derived. More than two thirds of the world's plant species - at least 35,000 of which are estimated to have medicinal value - come from the developing countries. At least 7,000 medical compounds in the modern pharmacopoeia are derived from plants

A survey released in May 2004 by the National Center for Complementary and Alternative Medicine focused on who used complementary and alternative medicines (CAM), what was used, and why it was used. The survey was limited to adults, aged 18 years and over during 2002, living in the United States.

According to this survey, herbal therapy, or use of natural products other than vitamins and minerals, was the most commonly used CAM therapy (18.9%) when all use of prayer was excluded.

Herbal remedies are very common in Europe. In Germany, herbal medications are dispensed by apothecaries. Prescription drugs are sold alongside essential oils, herbal extracts, or herbal teas. Herbal remedies are seen by some as a treatment to be preferred to pure medical compounds which have been industrially produced

In the United Kingdom, the training of medical herbalists is done by state funded Universities. For example, Bachelor of Science degrees in herbal medicine are offered at Universities such as University of East London, Middlesex University, University of Central Lancashire, University of Westminster, University of Lincoln and Napier University in Edinburgh at the present.

A 2004 Cochrane Collaboration review found that herbal therapies are supported by strong evidence but are not widely used in all clinical settings.

Herbal philosophy

There are four approaches to the use of plants as medicine:

1. The magical/shamanic

Almost all non-modern societies recognize this kind of use. The practitioner is regarded as endowed with gifts or powers that allow him/her to use herbs in a way that is hidden from the average person, and the herbs are said to affect the spirit or soul of the person.

2. The energetic

This approach includes the major systems of TCM (Traditional Chinese Medicine), Ayurveda, and Unani. Herbs are regarded as having actions in terms of their energies and affecting the energies of the body. The practitioner may have extensive training, and ideally be sensitive to energy, but need not have supernatural powers.

3. The functional dynamic

This approach was used by early physiomedical practitioners, whose doctrine forms the basis of contemporary practice in the UK. Herbs have a functional action, which is not necessarily linked to a physical compound, although often to a physiological function, but there is no explicit recourse to concepts involving energy.

4. The chemical

Modern practitioners - called Phytotherapists - attempt to explain herb actions in terms of their chemical constituents. It is generally assumed that the specific combination of secondary metabolites in the plant are responsible for the activity claimed or demonstrated, a concept called synergy.

Most modern herbalists concede that pharmaceuticals are more effective in emergency situations where time is of the essence. An example would be where a patient had an acute heart attack that posed imminent danger. However they claim that over the long term herbs can help the patient resist disease, and that in addition, they provide nutritional and immunological support that pharmaceuticals lack. They view their goal as prevention as well as cure.

Herbalists tend to use extracts from parts of plants, such as the roots or leaves but not isolate particular phytochemicals. Pharmaceutical medicine prefers single ingredients on the grounds that dosage can be more easily quantified. It is also possible to patent single compounds, and therefore generate income. Herbalists often reject the notion of a single active ingredient, arguing that the different phytochemicals present in many herbs will interact to enhance the therapeutic effects of the herb and dilute toxicity. Furthermore, they argue that a single ingredient may contribute to multiple effects. Herbalists deny that herbal synergism can be duplicated with synthetic chemicals. They argue that phytochemical interactions and trace components may alter the drug response in ways that cannot currently be replicated with a combination of a few putative active ingredients. Pharmaceutical researchers recognize the concept of drug synergism but note that clinical trials may be used to investigate the efficacy of a particular herbal preparation, provided the formulation of that herb is consistent.

In specific cases the claims of synergy and multi-functionality have been supported by science. The open question is how widely both can be generalized. Herbalists would argue that cases of synergy can be widely generalized, on the basis of their interpretation of evolutionary history, not necessarily shared by the pharmaceutical community. Plants are subject to similar selection pressures as humans and therefore they must develop resistance to threats such as radiation, reactive oxygen species and microbial attack in order to survive. Optimal chemical defenses have been selected for and have thus developed over millions of years. Human diseases are multi-factorial and may be treated by consuming the chemical defenses that they believe to be present in herbs. Bacteria, inflammation, nutrition and ROS (reactive oxygen species) may all play a role in arterial disease. Herbalists claim a single herb may simultaneously address several of these factors. Likewise a factor such as ROS may underlie more than one condition. In short herbalists view their field as the study of a web of relationships rather than a quest for single cause and a single cure for a single condition.

In selecting herbal treatments herbalists may use forms of information that are not applicable to pharmacists. Because herbs can moonlight as vegetables, teas or spices they have a huge consumer base and large-scale epidemiological studies become feasible. Ethnobotanical studies are another source of information. For example, when indigenous peoples from geographically dispersed areas use closely related herbs for the same purpose that is taken as supporting evidence for its efficacy. Herbalists contend that historical medical records and herbals are underutilized resources. They favor the use of convergent information in assessing the medical value of plants. An example would be when in-vitro activity is consistent with traditional use.

Figure 60 - Bełchatów Commune Coat of Arms showing a basket of Herbs & Grains

The Science

All plants produce chemical compounds as part of their normal metabolic activities. These are arbitrarily divided into primary metabolites, such as sugars and fats, found in all plants, and secondary metabolites, compounds not essential for basic function found in a smaller range of plants, some useful ones found only in a particular genus or species. Pigments harvest light, protect the organism from radiation and display colors to attract pollinators. Many common weeds, such as nettle, dandelion and chickweed, have medicinal properties.

The functions of secondary metabolites are varied. For example, some secondary metabolites are toxins used to deter predation, and others are pheromones used to attract insects for pollination. Phytoalexins protect against bacterial and fungal attacks. Allelochemicals inhibit rival plants that are competing for soil and light.

Plants upregulate and downregulate their biochemical paths in response to the local mix of herbivores, pollinators and microorganisms. The chemical profile of a single plant may vary over time as it reacts to changing conditions. It is the secondary metabolites and pigments that can have therapeutic actions in humans and which can be refined to produce drugs.

Plants synthesize a bewildering variety of phytochemicals but most are derivatives of a few biochemical motifs.

- **Alkaloids** contain a ring with nitrogen. Many alkaloids have dramatic effects on the central nervous system. Caffeine is an alkaloid that provides a mild lift but the alkaloids in datura cause severe intoxication and even death.
- **Phenolics** contain phenol rings. The anthocyanins that give grapes their purple color, the isoflavones, the phytoestrogens from soy and the tannins that give tea its astringency are phenolics.
- **Terpenoids** are built up from terpene building blocks. Each terpene consists of two paired isoprenes. The names

monoterpenes, sesquiterpenes, diterpenes and triterpenes are based on the number of isoprene units. The fragrance of rose and lavender is due to monoterpenes. The carotenoids produce the reds, yellows and oranges of pumpkin, corn and tomatoes.

- ✔ **Glycosides** consist of a glucose moiety attached to an aglycone. The aglycone is a molecule that is bioactive in its free form but inert until the glycoside bond is broken by water or enzymes. This mechanism allows the plant to defer the availability of the molecule to an appropriate time, similar to a safety lock on a gun. An example is the cyanoglycosides in cherry pits that release toxins only when bitten by a herbivore.

The word drug itself comes from the Dutch word "droog" (via the French word Drogue), which means 'dried plant'. Some examples are inulin from the roots of dahlias, quinine from the cinchona, morphine and codeine from the poppy, and digoxin from the foxglove.

The active ingredient in willow bark, once prescribed by Hippocrates, is salicin, which is converted in the body into salicylic acid. The discovery of salicylic acid would eventually lead to the development of the acetylated form acetylsalicylic acid, also known as "aspirin", when it was isolated from a plant known as meadowsweet. The word *aspirin* comes from an abbreviation of meadowsweet's Latin genus *Spiraea*, with an additional "A" at the beginning to acknowledge acetylation, and "in" was added at the end for easier pronunciation. "Aspirin" was originally a brand name, and is still a protected trademark in some countries. This medication was patented by Bayer AG.

Methods of administration

There are many forms in which herbs can be administered, these include:

- **Tinctures** - Alcoholic extracts of herbs such as Echinacea extract. Usually obtained by combining 100% pure ethanol (or a mixture of 100% ethanol with water) with the herb. A completed tincture has a ethanol percentage of at least 25% (sometimes up to 90%). The term tincture is sometimes applied to preparations using other solvents than ethanol.

- **Herbal wine and elixirs** - These are alcoholic extract of herbs; usually with an ethanol percentage of 12-38% Herbal wine is a maceration of herbs in wine, while an elixir is a maceration of herbs in spirits (e.g., vodka, grappa, etc.)

- **Tisanes** - Hot water extracts of herb, such as chamomile.

- **Decoctions** - Long-term boiled extract of usually roots or bark.

- **Macerates** - Cold infusion of plants with high mucilage-content as sage, thyme, etc. Plants are chopped and added to cold water. They are then left to stand for 7 to 12 hours (depending on herb used). For most macerates 10 hours is used.

- **Vinegars** - Prepared the same way as tinctures, except using a solution of acetic acid as the solvent.

- **Whole herb consumption** - This can occur in either dried form (herbal powder), or fresh juice, (fresh leaves and other plant parts).

- **Syrups** - Extracts of herbs made with syrup or honey. Sixty five parts of sugar are mixed with 35 parts of water and herb. The whole is then boiled and macerated for three weeks.

- ✔ **Extracts** - Include liquid extracts, dry extracts and nebulisates[18]. Liquid extracts are liquids with a lower ethanol percentage than tinctures. They can (and are usually) made by vacuum distilling tinctures. Dry extracts are extracts of plant material which are evaporated into a dry mass. They can then be further refined to a capsule or tablet.

- ✔ **Inhalation** as in **aromatherapy** can be used as a mood changing treatmen' to fight a sinus infection or cough, or to cleanse the skin on a deeper level (steam rather than direct inhalation here).

- ✔ **Topicals:**

  - ✿ **Essential oils** - Application of essential oil extracts, usually diluted in a carrier oil (many essential oils can burn the skin or are simply too high dose used straight – diluting in olive oil or another food grade oil such as almond oil can allow these to be used safely as a topical).

  - ✿ **Salves, oils, balms, creams and lotions** - Most topical applications are oil extractions of herbs. Taking a food grade oil and soaking herbs in it for anywhere from weeks to months allows certain phytochemicals to be extracted into the oil. This oil can then be made into salves, creams, lotions, or simply used as an oil for topical application. Any massage oils, antibacterial salves and wound healing compounds are made this way.

  - ✿ **Poultices and compresses** - One can also make a poultice or compress using whole herb (or the appropriate part of the plant) usually crushed or dried and re-hydrated with a small amount of water and then applied directly in a bandage, cloth or just as is.

---

[18] A nebulisate is a dry extract created by freeze-drying and admininstered by a device – such as an inhaler used to treast asthma

Anglo-Saxon Sources

There are several extant Anglo-Saxon sources for herbal lore and leechcraft[19] in general.

- 🌿 The Lacnunga Manuscript
- 🌿 The Old English Herbarium Manuscript V
- 🌿 Bald's *Leechbook* – Book III
- 🌿 The Omont Fragment

Stephen Pollington's excellent book *Leechcraft – Early English Charms, Plantlore and Healing,* contains fully translated versions and notes on the first three sources listed above.

In his introduction to the translation of the *Omont fragment* on Northvegr.com, Justin Bullard has the following to say:

"The Omont Fragment is one small leaf of text but its importance as a contribution to Anglo-Saxon domestic medicine is tremendous. Our lesson here is that before dismissing domestic medical treatments, from any medical tradition, we should realize that prior to pharmaceutical companies and the technology to synthesize chemicals, we had to rely on plants to obtain our drugs (and still do in many cases). Respecting local medical knowledge and setting aside our biases will enable us to appreciate the wisdom of the ancients."

In the following section on natural remedies, all of the plants, herbs and substances described, were used and attested in the above mentioned Anglo-Saxon sources.

---

[19] The art of healing; skill of a physician.

Be happy while you're living, For you're a long time dead.
- Scottish Proverb

Natural Remedies

In the following pages I will present Ten remedies used by our ancestors as described in the old Anglo-Saxon manuscripts, and updated with any relevant modern infromation.

I will follow up with a Book dedicated to Northern herbal remedies, but for now, lets explore a small sample.

Chamomile (German)

Matricaria recutita

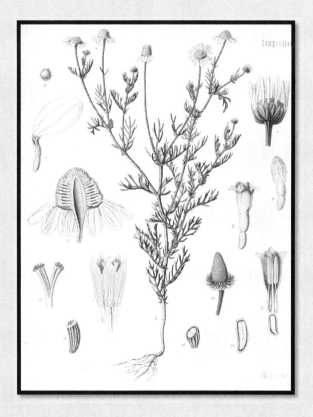

Plant family: Asteraceae (Daisy family)

Part used: Flower

Taste: Bitter, spicy

Historical Notes: Use of Chamomile dates back as far as ancient Egypt where it was dedicated to their gods.

English Chamomile (a close relative) was known as Maythe – derived from the word for Maiden, and was used to treat woman's period pains.

Actions: Antiseptic, antibiotic, disinfectant, bactericidal & vermifuge

Modern findings: "Chamomile tea, perhaps the best-known herbal tisane, is widely employed as a digestive remedy throughout Europe, and its therapeutic use is well documented," says David Hoffman, author of Medical Herbalism. The herb relaxes spasms of the smooth muscles and counters inflammation in the gut lining; it also has antiseptic and vasodilatory effects.

Preparations: Tisane: It's important to use water that is very hot but not boiling because boiling water can destroy the therapeutic properties of the Chamomile herb. If you prefer using loose dried Chamomile add **two teaspoons** of it to an individual tea infuser. Add the infuser, or a teabag if you're using this instead, to your cup and pour in the heated water. Let it **steep for about five minutes** and then it's ready to drink.

Active constituents: Terpene bisabolol, farnesene, chamazulene, flavonoids (including apigenin, quercetin, patuletin and luteolin), coumarin, essential oils (up to 2%), mucilage (a slippery material comprised of polysaccharides and other ingredients; up to 10%), and coumarins (up to 0.1%).

Flavonoids and essential oils often produce antispasmodic and anti-inflammatory effects for the gastrointestinal system and are likely to be the main active constituents.

Cautions: Allergic reactions are possible, especially if you're sensitive to ragweed.

English Oak

Quercus robur

Plant family: Fagaceae

Part used: Bark

Taste: Bitter

Historical Notes: In Celtic mythology, it is the tree of doors, believed to be a gateway between worlds, or a place where portals could be erected.

In Norse mythology, the oak was sacred to the thunder god, Thor. Some scholars speculate that this is because the oak, as the largest tree in northern Europe, was the one most often struck by lightning. Thor's Oak was a sacred tree of the Germanic Chatti tribe. Its destruction marked the Christianisation of the heathen tribes by the Franks.

Actions: anti-inflammatory, antiseptic, astringent, tonic, vulnerary

Modern findings: Oak Bark may be used wherever a strong astringent is indicated, for example in unresponsive diarrhoea or dysentery. However, with its high tannin content it might be too strong in some situations, causing constipation. As a gargle it can be used in tonsillitis, pharyngitis and laryngitis. As an enema it is used for the treatment of haemorrhoids and as a douche for leucorrhoea. It's primary indication is acute diarrhoea, take infrequent small doses.

Oak bark is also rich in tannin, and is used by tanners for tanning leather. Acorns are used for making flour or roasted for acorn coffee. Oak galls were used for centuries as the main ingredient in manuscript ink, harvested at a specific time of year.

Preparations: Decoction: put 1 teaspoonful of the bark in a cup of water, bring to the boil and simmer gently for 10-15 minutes. This can be drunk three times a day. Tincture: take 1-2 ml of the tincture three times a day.

Active constituents: The whole complex of primary plant constituents and acharacteristic array of secondary plant constituents are present. The 15-20% tannins produce the dominant pharmacological effects.

Cautions: none known for the bark, but acorns can be toxic

Feverfew

Tanacetum parthenium

Plant family: Asteraceae (Daisy family)

Part used: Leaves

Taste: Bitter

Historical Notes: The word "feverfew" derives from the Latin febrifugia, meaning "fever reducer."

Actions: Used for reducing fever, for prevention of migraine headaches, arthritis and digestive problems.

Modern findings: The migraine-relieving activity of feverfew is believed to be due to parthenolide, an active compound that helps relieve smooth muscle spasms. In particular, it helps prevent the constriction of blood vessels in the brain (one of the leading causes of migraine headaches). Parthenolide also inhibits the actions of compounds that cause inflammation and may inhibit cancer cell growth.

Preparations & Dosage: Leaf (dried) - Around 75 mg of dried leaves may be taken daily for arthritis relief. For migraine relief, 2-3 leaves may be taken daily, during or after meals. Leaf (fresh) - For migraine relief, 2-3 leaves may be taken daily, during or after meals.

For migraine headaches: Take 100 - 300 mg, up to 4 times daily, standardized to contain 0.2 - 0.4% parthenolides. Feverfew may be used to prevent or stop a migraine headache. Feverfew supplements may also be carbon dioxide extracted. For these, take 6.25 mg, 3 times daily, for up to 16 weeks.

For inflammatory conditions (such as arthritis): 120 - 60 drops, 2 times daily of a 1:1 w/v fluid extract, or 60 - 120 drops 2 times daily of 1:5 w/v tincture.

Active constituents: parthenolide, tanetin and melatonin.

Cautions: If feverfew is taken for any length of time as a medicinal herb, sudden discontinuation can result in a withdrawal syndrome consisting of headache, irritability, trouble sleeping and joint pain. Feverfew may alter the effects of some prescription and nonprescription medications. If you are currently being treated with any of the following medications, you should not use feverfew without first talking to your health care provider.

It is contraindicated in pregnancy.

Garlic

Allium sativum

Plant family: Alliaceae

Part used: Bulbs / Cloves

Taste: Pungent and spicy

Historical Notes: Garlic has been used as both food and medicine in many cultures for thousands of years, dating at least as far back as the time that the Giza pyramids were built. It was consumed by ancient Greek and Roman soldiers, sailors, and rural folk.

Garleac derives it's name directly from Old English, where *gar* signifies a spear, and *leac*, any kind of muli-layered onion-like vegetable.

Actions: antibiotic, antispetic, antihistamine, anticoagulant, expectorant, antiparasitic, alterative, diaphoretic, diuretic, stimulant, and antispasmodic.

Modern findings: The key therapeutic ingredient in garlic is alliin. Alliin is an odorless sulfur-containing chemical derived from the amino acid cysteine. Allicin is formed when alliin, a sulfur-containing amino acid, comes into contact with the enzyme alliinase when raw garlic is chopped, crushed, or chewed. Allicin is what gives garlic its antibiotic properties and is responsible for its strong odor. Allicin is said to be stronger than penicillin and tetracycline, and microbes do not mutate when repeatedly exposed to garlic. Allicin is further broken down to a compound called ajoene. Ajoene contritrbutes to the anticoagulant action of garlic

Preparations & Dosage:

- Whole garlic clove (as a food supplement): 2 - 4 grams per day of fresh, minced garlic clove (each clove is approximately 1 gram).
- Aged garlic extract: 600 - 1,200 mg, daily in divided doses.
- Tablets of freeze-dried garlic: 200 mg, 2 tablets 3 times daily, standardized to 1.3% alliin or 0.6% allicin. Products may also be found standardized to contain 10 - 12 mg/Gm alliin and 4,000 mcg of total allicin potential (TAP). Fluid extract (1:1 w/v): 4 mL, daily. Tincture (1:5 w/v): 20 mL, daily. Oil: 0.03 - 0.12 mL, 3 times daily

Active constituents: Garlic contains many active constituents, including volatile oil with sulphur-containing compounds (allicin, alliin, and ajoene), enzymes (allinase, peroxidase and myrosinase), glucokinins, B group vitamins, vitamin C and flavonoids, citral, geraniol, linalool, aphellandrene and B phellandrene. Garlic also contains a wide range of trace minerals. These include copper, iron, zinc, magnesium, germanium, and selenium.

Cautions: none known

Honey

Mel Millis

Part used: Syrup

Taste: Sweet

Historical Notes: Honey collection is an ancient activity dating back at least 10,000 years ago. In Ancient Egypt, honey was used to sweeten cakes and biscuits, and was used in many other dishes. Ancient Egyptian and Middle-Eastern peoples also used honey for embalming the dead. In the Roman Empire, honey was possibly used instead of gold to pay taxes. For at least 2700 years, honey has been used by humans to treat a variety of ailments through topical application, but only recently have the antiseptic and antibacterial properties of honey been chemically explained.

Actions: Antibacterial, antimicrobial,

Modern findings: Wound gels that contain antibacterial raw honey and have regulatory approval for wound care are now available to help conventional medicine in the battle against drug resistant strains of bacteria MRSA. As an antimicrobial agent honey may have the potential for treating a variety of ailments. Antibacterial properties of honey are the result of the low water activity causing osmosis, hydrogen peroxide effect, high acidity, and the antibacterial activity of methylglyoxal. Honey appears to be effective in killing drug-resistant biofilms which are implicated in chronic rhinosinusitis.

When honey is used topically (as, for example, a wound dressing), hydrogen peroxide is produced by dilution of the honey with body fluids. As a result, hydrogen peroxide is released slowly and acts as an antiseptic.

"Honey is cheap, making it potentially useful for treating wounds in earthquake-stricken and war-torn areas where running water is scarce and often contaminated. It is being used in Iraq to treat burn wounds in children." - Unknown

Preparations & Dosage: As an anti-septic, apply honey to the wound or burn before bandaging.

Active constituents: glucose, fructose, minerals like magnesium, potassium, calcium, sodium chlorine, sulphur, iron and phosphate. It contains vitamins B1, B2, C, B6, B5 and B3 all of which change according to the qualities of the nectar and pollen. Besides the above, copper, iodine, and zinc exist in it in small quantities.

Cautions: Infant botulism is a rare but serious paralytic disease caused by the microorganism Clostridium botulinum. The National Honey Board, along with other health organizations, recommends that honey not be fed to infants under one year of age

Salt

Sali

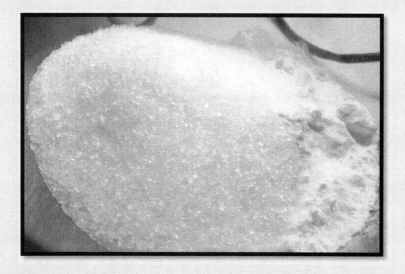

Taste: Salty

Historical Notes: *Wich* and *wych* are names used to denote brine springs or wells in England. Originally derived from the Latin vicus, meaning place, by the 11th century use of the 'wich' suffix in placenames was associated with towns with salt production. Several English places carry the suffix and are historically related to salt, including the four Cheshire 'wiches' of Middlewich, Nantwich, Northwich and Leftwich (a small village south of Northwich), and Droitwich in Worcestershire.

Following the Roman invasion, Middlewich was named Salinae due to the salt deposits around it, as it was one of their major sites of salt production.

Hippocrates encouraged his fellow healers to make use of salt water to heal various ailments by immersing their patients in sea water.

Actions: Disinfectant

Modern findings: When you have a bacterial or viral infection in your throat and you gargle with saltwater, the water drains into your body, but some of the salt stays on the surface of your throat. There it attaches to the infectious cells and draws out the moisture inside the cells, effectively dehydrating them until they are dried up and dead.

The same thing happens when you put salt water on your skin. As the water evaporates, leaving the salt behind, it attaches to the surface of infectious cells, draws the moisture out, and kills the cells.

Preparations & Dosage:

- Sore Throat: The simplest remedy for minor sore throat pain is a warm saltwater gargle (no matter how much you dislike the taste!). Just add 1 teaspoon salt to 8 ounces warm water, and gargle several times a day. See a physician if the sore throat persists longer than 3 days or is accompanied by a high fever.
- Burns or Injuries: A severe burn in your mouth from eating something very hot can be relieved by rinsing with saltwater every hour or so. Use 1/2 teaspoon salt in 8 ounces warm water.
- Gums: Swish with 1 teaspoon salt in 4 ounces warm water when gums are painful. If you have an abscess, the salt will draw out some of the infection. Any gum pain should be treated by a dentist as soon as possible.
- Toothaches: As a temporary remedy for a toothache before going to the dentist, rinse your mouth with a mixture of 4 ounces warm water, 2 tablespoons vinegar, and 1 tablespoon salt.
- Bee stings and bug bites: Combine equal parts baking soda and salt, then brush onto a sting or bite area to help relieve itch.
- Treat a mosquito bite by soaking it for a few minutes in saltwater, then applying an ointment made of salt and lard.
- Poison ivy and poison oak: Help poison ivy clear up more quickly by soaking irritated skin in hot saltwater.

St. Johns Wort

Hypericum peforatum

Plant family: Hypericaceae (Hypericum family)

Part used: The flowers

Taste: Bitter

Historical Notes: Mentioned in the OE *Herbarium* as *hypericon*. This plant was gathered on the eve of St. Johns day (June 24'th) roughly coincinding with the summer solstice.

Though long used, this herb was a relatively minor one in the European tradition until the latter part of the 20th century when its antidepressant activities were researched and shown to be significant.

Actions: Sedative for depression, anxiety, irritability, nervous tension.

Modern findings: This herb has become one of the most intensively investigated in modern times due to the possibility that it acts as a safer but equally effective antidepressant when compared to several modern drug therapies.

Preparations & Dosage: Add 1 to 2 cups of St John's Wort flowers to 1 cup of boiling water, simmer, strain and drink. The recommended St John's Wort dosage for tea is up to three times per day, while the recommended dosage for St John's Wort tincture is ¼ teaspoon to 1 teaspoon, up to three times daily.

It is recommended that one examines St John's Wort's effectiveness after about 4 to 6 weeks before continuing with further consumption.

Active constituents: Tannins (similar to those found in tea), flavonoids, volatile oils, and hypericin, a complex flavonoid that is used as a measure for standardized extracts (though it is not believed to be the main active component).

Cautions: Photosensitization is possible, though rare; interactions with some drugs may occur (these include: Warfarin, serotonin-uptake inhibitors, digitoxin, theophylline, cyclosporin, phenprocoumon, Indinavir, oral contraceptives), though the dosage of St. John's Wort used here should have minimal effects even when taking the full dose of 1 teabag three times per day.

Stinging Nettle

Urtica dioica

Plant family: Urticaceae

Part used: Leaves, Stem and Root

Taste: Bitter

Historical Notes: As Old English Stiðe, nettle is one of the nine plants invoked in the pagan Anglo-Saxon Nine Herbs Charm, recorded in the 10th century. In medieval Europe, it was used as a diuretic (to rid the body of excess water) and to treat joint pain.

Actions: Astringent, diuretic and tonic

Modern findings: Nettle leaf has a long tradition in the treatment of arthritis in Germany. Nettle leaf extract contains active compounds that reduce TNF-α and other inflammatory cytokines. It has been demonstrated that nettle leaf lowers TNF-α levels by potently inhibiting the genetic transcription factor that activates TNF-α and IL-1B in the synovial tissue that lines the joint. Nettle root extracts have been extensively studied in human clinical trials as a treatment for symptoms of benign prostatic hyperplasia (BPH). These extracts have been shown to help relieve symptoms compared to placebo both by themselves and when combined with other herbal medicines.

Preparations & Dosage:

- Tisane: prepare by pouring 2/3 cup of boiling water over 3 - 4 tsp of dried leaves or dried root and steeping for 3 - 5 minutes. Drink 3 - 4 cups per day. You can also make an infusion with fresh nettle leaves. Always drink additional water along with the tea.
- Dried leaf: 2 - 4 grams, 3 times a day.
- Fluid extract (root,1:1): 1.5 mL, 3 - 4 times daily.
- Fluid extract (leaf, 1:1): 2 - 5 mL 3 times daily.
- Tincture (root, 1:5): 1 - 4 mL 3 - 4 times daily.

Active constituents: The leaves contain minerals, amines, flavonol glycosides, phenolic acids, scopoletin, b-sitosterol, as well as tannins, while the roots contain polysaccharides, a lectin, phenolics, sterols and their glycosides.

Cautions: Occasional side effects include mild stomach upset, fluid retention, and hives or rash (mainly from topical use). It is important to be careful when handling the nettle plant because touching it can cause an allergic rash. Stinging nettle should never be applied to an open wound. Because nettle can alter the menstrual cycle and may contribute to miscarriage, pregnant women should not use nettle.

Willow Bark

Salix

Plant family: Salicaceae

Part used: Bark & Leaves

Taste: Bitter

Historical Notes: Has been in use for aprox. 6000yrs and was described in the 1st century CE by Dioscorides. The leaves and bark of the willow tree have been mentioned in ancient texts from Assyria, Sumer and Egypt as a remedy for aches and fever, and the Ancient Greek physician Hippocrates wrote about its medicinal properties in the 5th century BC.

Actions: Bitter tonic, astringent, styptic, analgesic, anti-inflammatory, antipyretic

Modern findings:

Preparations & Dosage :

- Tisane: 1 - 2 tsp of dried bark in a cup of water (250 ml)
- Fresh Plant Tincture: catkins, leaves, bark, 1:2, 95% alcohol, 3-60 gtt
- Dry Plant Tincture: dried bark, 1:5, 1-5 mL
- Cold Infusion: fresh aerial parts, 1:20, 200 mL
- Decoction: catkins, bark, 1:20, 60-90 mL
- Powder: 3-5 g

Active constituents: Willow contains glycosides, tannins, salicylic acid, catechins and flavonoids.

Cautions: As with aspirin, some people may experience stomach upset from taking willow. Although such symptoms are less likely from willow than from aspirin, people with ulcers and gastritis should, nevertheless, avoid this herb. Again, as with aspirin, willow should not be used to treat fevers in children since it may cause Reye's syndrome.

Valerian

Valeriana officinalis

Plant family: Valerianaceae

Part used: The rhizomes, roots, and essential oil

Taste: Spicy & Bitter

Historical Notes: Valerian has been used as a medicinal herb since at least the time of ancient Greece and Rome. Hippocrates described its properties, and Galen later prescribed it as a remedy for insomnia. In medieval Sweden, it was sometimes placed in the wedding clothes of the groom to ward off the "envy" of the elves

Actions: Sedative, nervine relaxant, antispasmodic, hypotensive, anodyne, carminative

Modern findings: Valerian has a fairly wide range of uses in the home medicine cabinet. It is an effective stress reducer, and has benefit in cases of nervous tension, depression, irritability, hysteria, panic, anxiety, fear, stomach cramping, indigestion due to nervousness, delusions, exhaustion, and, of course, nervous sleeplessness. It also appears to have real benefits in cases of sciatica, multiple sclerosis, epilepsy, shingles, and peripheral neuropathy, including numbness, tingling, muscle weakness, and pain in the extremities. Testing has also revealed that it eases muscle cramping, rheumatic pain, migraines, uterine cramps, intestinal colic, and stress-related heart problems and hypertension. It has shown some benefit in behavioral problems in both adults and children, and is used to treat attention deficit disorders, hyperactivity, anxiety headaches, and bedwetting, and it has shown some promise in helping reduce thumb sucking and nail biting in children. It has a stabilizing effect on blood pressure and can help regulate arrhythmias. Lastly, Valerian is useful as a digestive aid, is helpful in cases of gas, diarrhea, and cramps, and alleviates the pain of ulcers. In the respiratory tract, it is believed to be of benefit in reducing the discomfort of asthma attacks.

Preparations & Dosage: The usual dose with an oil is 1 teaspoon as needed, and with a tea or capsule, 1-2 cups or tablets as needed. Prepare valerian tea in the morning by adding 2 tsp. of valerian root to 2 cups of warm water. Let stand until the evening. Strain and warm. Add 1 tsp. of honey and drink 1 cup after dinner and 1 cup before going to bed.

Active constituents: Alkaloids, Isovaleramide, Gamma-aminobutyric acid, Valeric acid, Valepotriates, acevaltrate, isovaltrate and valtrate, Volatile oil containing active sesquiterpenes (acetoxyvalerenic acid, valerenic acid) and Flavanones such as hesperidin, 6-methylapigenin and linarin

Cautions: Valerian is contraindicated in pregnant and breast feeding women, but otherwise is a safe herb to use intermittently

Spread the table and contention will cease.
- *English Proverb*

Chapter 6 – Northern Cuisine

lthough our ancestors had access to fewer ingredients than do modern chefs, they nevertheless enjoyed a great variety of food and drink; relying on available ingredients such as herbs like dill, coriander, hops, black mustard and fennel to flavor, and honey to sweeten. In this chapter we'll explore a sampling of interesting and savory recipes, and delve into the lore of the most famous of Northern beverages – Mead.

The Mead of Poetry

There's more to mead than it's obvious consumption as an alcoholic beverage. Mead is one of the corner stones of Northern Mythology; the Poetic Mead or Mead of Poetry, also known as Mead of Suttungr, is a mythical beverage that whoever "drinks becomes a skald or scholar" to recite any information and solve any question.. The drink is a vivid metaphor for poetic inspiration, often associated with Odin the god of 'possession' via berserkr rage or poetic inspiration. Let's explore the mythology behind mead.

Creation of the mead and murder of Kvasir

The Aesir had a dispute with the folk which are called Vanir, and they appointed a peace-meeting between them and established peace in this way: they each went to a vat and spat their spittle therein. Then at parting the gods took that peace token and would not let it perish, but shaped thereof a man. This man is called **Kvasir**, and he was so wise that none could question him concerning anything but that he knew the solution. He went up and down the earth to give instruction to men; and when he came upon invitation to the abode of certain dwarves, Fjalar and Gjallar, they called him into privy converse with them, and killed him, letting his blood run into two vats and a kettle. The kettle is named Odrerir, and the vats Son and Bodn; they blended honey with the blood, and the outcome was that mead by the virtue of which he who drinks becomes a skald or scholar. The dwarves reported to the Aesir that Kvasir had choked on his own shrewdness, since there was none so wise there as to be able to question his wisdom. Then these dwarves invited the giant who is called Gilling to visit them, and his wife with him. Next the dwarves invited Gilling to row upon the sea with them; but when they had gone out from the land, the dwarves rowed into the breakers and capsized the boat. Gillingr was unable to swim, and he

perished; but the dwarves righted their boat and rowed to land. They reported this accident to his wife, but she took it grievously and wept aloud. Then Fjalar asked her whether it would ease her heart if she should look out upon the sea at the spot where he had perished; and she desired it. Then he spoke softly to Gjallar his brother, bidding him go up over the doorway, when she should go out, and let a mill-stone fall on her head, saying that her weeping grew wearisome to him; and so he did.

Now when the giant Suttung, Gilling's son, learned of

GIANT SUTTUNG AND THE DWARFS.

Figure 61 - Suttung

this, he went over and took the dwarves and carried them out to sea, and set them on a reef which was covered at high tide. They besought Suttungr to grant them respite of their lives, and as the price of reconciliation offered him the precious mead in satisfaction of his father's death. And that became a means of reconciliation between them. Suttungr carried the mead home and concealed it in the place called Hnitbjorg, placing his daughter Gunnlod there to watch over it.

Because of this we call poetry Kvasir's Blood or Dwarves' Drink, or Ferry-Boat of Dwarves — since this mead brought them life-ransom from the reef—or Suttungr's Mead, or Liquor of Hnitbjorg.

Odin Acquires the Mead

Odin departed from home and came to a certain place where nine thralls were mowing hay. He asked if they desired him to whet their scythes, and they assented. Then he took a hone from his belt and whetted the scythes; it seemed to them that the scythes cut better by far, and they asked that the hone be sold them. But he put such a value on it that whoso desired to buy must give a considerable price: nonetheless all said that they would agree, and prayed him to sell it to them. He cast the hone up into the air; but since all wished to lay their hands on it, they became so intermingled with one another that each struck with his scythe against the other's neck.

Odin sought a night's lodging with the giant who is called Baugi, Suttung's brother. Baugi bewailed his husbandry, saying that his nine thralls had killed one another, and declared that he had no hope of workmen. Odin called himself Bölverk[20] in Baugi's presence; he offered to undertake nine men's work for Baugi, and demanded for his wages one drink of Suttung's Mead. Baugi declared that he had no control whatever over the mead, and said that Suttung was determined to have it to himself, but promised to go with Bölverk and try if they might get the mead. During the summer Bölverk accomplished nine men's work for Baugi, but when winter came he asked Baugi for his hire. Then they both set out for Suttung's.

---

[20] Meaning Bale Worker

Baugi told Suttung his brother of his bargain with Bölverk; but Suttung flatly refused them a single drop of the mead. Then Bölverk made suggestion to Baugi that they try certain wiles, if perchance they might find means to get at the mead; and Baugi agreed readily. Thereupon Bölverk drew out the auger called Rati, saying that Baugi must bore the rock, if the auger cut. He did so. At last Baugi said that the rock was bored through, but Bölverk blew into the auger-hole, and the chips flew up at him. Then he discovered that Baugi would have deceived him, and he bade him bore through the rock. Baugi bored anew; and when Bölverk blew a second time, then the chips were blown in by the blast. Then Bölverk turned himself into a serpent and crawled into the auger-hole, but Baugi thrust at him from behind with the auger and missed him. Bölverk proceeded to the place where Gunnlöd was, and lay with her three nights; and then she gave him leave to drink three draughts of the mead. In the first draught he drank every drop out of Odrerir; and in the second, he emptied Bodn; and in the third, Son; and then he had all the mead. Then he turned himself into the shape of an eagle and flew as furiously as he could; but when Suttung saw the eagle's flight, he too assumed the fashion of an eagle and flew after him. When the Aesir saw Odin flying, straightway they set out their vats in the court; and when Odin came into Asgard, he spat up the mead into the vats. Nevertheless he came so near to being caught by Suttung that he sent some mead backwards, and no heed was taken of this: whosoever would might have that, and we call that the poetaster's part. But Odin gave the mead of Suttungr to the Aesir and to those men who possess the ability to compose.

Therefore we call poetry, Odin's Booty and Find, and his Drink and Gift, and the Drink of the Aesir.

Mead as a Beverage

Mead is an alcoholic beverage, made from honey and water via fermentation with yeast. It's alcoholic content may range from that of a mild ale to that of a strong wine. It may be still, carbonated, or sparkling; it may be dry, semi-sweet, or sweet. Mead is often referred to as "honey wine."

Depending on local traditions and specific recipes, it may be brewed with spices, fruits, or grain mash. It may be produced by fermentation of honey with grain mash; mead may also be flavored with hops to produce a bitter, beer-like flavor.

Figure 62 - Honey

Mead is independently multicultural. It is known from many sources of ancient history throughout Europe, Africa and Asia, although archaeological evidence of it is ambiguous. Its origins are lost in prehistory; "it can be regarded as the ancestor of all fermented drinks," Maguelonne Toussaint-Samat has observed, "antedating the cultivation of the soil."Claude Lévi-Strauss makes a case for the invention of mead as a marker of the passage "from nature to culture."

The earliest archaeological evidence for the production of mead dates to around 7000 BC. Pottery vessels containing a mixture of mead, rice and other fruits along with organic compounds of fermentation were found in Northern China. In Europe, it is first attested in residual samples found in the characteristic ceramics of the Bell Beaker Culture.

The earliest surviving description of mead is in the hymns of the Rigveda, one of the sacred books of the historical Vedic religion and (later) Hinduism dated around 1700–1100 BC. During the Golden Age of Ancient Greece, mead was said to be the preferred drink. Aristotle (384–322 BC) discussed mead in his Meteorologica and elsewhere, while Pliny the Elder (AD 23–79) called mead militites in his Naturalis Historia and differentiated wine sweetened with honey or "honey-wine" from mead. The Spanish-Roman naturalist Columella gave a recipe for mead in De re rustica, about AD 60.

Around AD 550, the Brythonic speaking bard Taliesin wrote the Kanu y med or "Song of Mead." The legendary drinking, feasting and boasting of warriors in the mead hall is echoed in the mead hall Dyn Eidyn (modern day Edinburgh), and in the epic poem Y Gododdin, both dated around AD 700. In the Old English epic poem Beowulf, the Danish warriors drank Honey mead. Mead was the historical beverage par excellence and commonly brewed by the Germanic tribes in Northern Europe. Later, heavy taxation and regulations governing the ingredients of alcoholic beverages led to commercial mead becoming a more obscure beverage until recently. Some monasteries kept up the old traditions of mead-making as a by-product of beekeeping, especially in areas where grapes could not be grown.

Mead was also popular in Central Europe and in the Baltic states. In the Polish language mead is called miód pitny, meaning "drinkable honey." In Russia mead remained popular as medovukha and sbiten long after its decline in the West. Sbiten is often mentioned in the works of 19th-century Russian writers, including Gogol, Dostoevsky and Tolstoy.

Varieties

Mead can have a wide range of flavors, depending on the source of the honey, additives (also known as "adjuncts" or "gruit"), including fruit and spices, the yeast employed during fermentation, and aging procedure. Some producers have marketed white wine with added honey as mead, often spelling it "meade." This is closer in style to a Hypocras. Blended varieties of mead may be known by either style represented. For instance, a mead made with cinnamon and apples may be referred to as either a cinnamon **cyser** or an apple metheglin.

A mead that also contains spices (such as cloves, cinnamon or nutmeg), or herbs (such as oregano, hops, or even lavender or chamomile), is called a **metheglin**.

A mead that contains fruit (such as raspberry, blackberry or strawberry) is called a melomel, which was also used as a means of food preservation, keeping summer produce for the winter. A mead that is fermented with grape juice is called a **pyment**.

Mulled mead is a popular drink at Christmas time, where mead is flavored with spices (and sometimes various fruits) and warmed, traditionally by having a hot poker plunged into it.

Some meads retain some measure of the sweetness of the original honey, and some may even be considered dessert wines. Drier meads are also available, and some producers offer sparkling meads. There are a number of faux-meads, which are actually cheap wines with large amounts of honey added, to produce a cloyingly sweet liqueur.

Historically, meads were fermented by wild yeasts and bacteria (as noted in the below quoted recipe) residing on the skins of the fruit or within the honey itself. Wild yeasts generally provide inconsistent results, and in modern times various brewing interests have isolated the strains now in use. Certain strains have gradually become associated with certain styles of mead. Mostly, these are strains that are also used in beer or wine production. However, several commercial labs, such as White Labs, WYeast, Vierka, have developed yeast strains specifically for mead. Mead yeasts are better suited to preserve the delicate honey flavors than a wine or beer yeast.

Mead can be distilled to a brandy or liqueur strength. Krupnik is a sweet Polish liqueur made through such a process. A version of this called "honey jack" can be made by partly freezing a quantity of mead and pouring off the liquid without the ice crystals (a process known as freeze distillation), in the same way that applejack is made from cider.

Mead variants

- **Acan** — A Native Mexican version of mead.
- **Acerglyn** — A mead made with honey and maple syrup.
- **Bochet** — A mead where the honey is caramelized or burned separately before adding the water. Gives toffee, chocolate, marshmallow flavors.
- **Braggot** — Braggot (also called bracket or brackett). Originally brewed with honey and hops, later with honey and malt — with or without hops added. Welsh origin (bragawd).
- **Black mead** — A name sometimes given to the blend of honey and blackcurrants.
- **Capsicumel** — A mead flavored with chile peppers.
- **Chouchenn** — A kind of mead made in Brittany.
- **Cyser** — A blend of honey and apple juice fermented together; see also cider.
- **Czwórniak** — A Polish mead, made using three units of water for each unit of honey
- **Dandaghare** — A mead from Nepal, combines honey with Himalayan herbs and spices. It has been brewed since 1972 in the city of Pokhara.
- **Dwójniak** — A Polish mead, made using equal amounts of water and honey
- **Great mead** — Any mead that is intended to be aged several years. The designation is meant to distinguish this type of mead from "short mead" (see below).
- **Gverc or Medovina** — Croatian mead prepared in Samobor and many other places. The word "gverc" or "gvirc" is from the German "Gewürze" and refers to various spices added to mead.
- **Hydromel** — Hydromel literally means "water-honey" in Greek. It is also the French name for mead. (Compare with the Spanish hidromiel and aquamiel, Italian idromele and Portuguese hidromel). It is also used as a name for a very light or low-alcohol mead.
- **Medica** — Slovenian, Croatian, variety of Mead.
- **Medovina** — Czech, Serbian, Bulgarian, Bosnian and Slovak for mead. Commercially available in Czech Republic, Slovakia and presumably other Central and Eastern European countries.
- **Medovukha** — Eastern Slavic variant (honey-based fermented drink)
- **Melomel** — Melomel is made from honey and any fruit. Depending on the fruit-base used, certain melomels may also be known by more specific names (see cyser, pyment, morat for examples)

- **Metheglin** — Metheglin starts with traditional mead but has herbs and/or spices added. Some of the most common metheglins are ginger, tea, orange peel, nutmeg, coriander, cinnamon, cloves or vanilla. Its name indicates that many metheglins were originally employed as folk medicines. The Welsh word for mead is medd, and the word "metheglin" derives from meddyglyn, a compound of meddyg, "healing" + llyn, "liquor."
- **Morat** — Morat blends honey and mulberries.
- **Mulsum** — Mulsum is not a true mead, but is unfermented honey blended with a high-alcohol wine.
- **Omphacomel** — A mediæval mead recipe that blends honey with verjuice; could therefore be considered a variety of pyment (qv).
- **Oxymel** — Another historical mead recipe, blending honey with wine vinegar.
- **Pitarrilla** — Mayan drink made from a fermented mixture of wild honey, balché tree bark and fresh water.
- **Pyment** — Pyment blends honey and red or white grapes. Pyment made with white grape juice is sometimes called "white mead."
- **Półtorak** — A Polish mead, made using two units of honey for each unit of water
- **Rhodomel** — Rhodomel is made from honey, rose hips, petals or rose attar and water.
- **Sack mead** — This refers to mead that is made with more copious amounts of honey than usual. The finished product retains an extremely high specific gravity and elevated levels of sweetness. It derives its name, according to one theory, from the fortified dessert wine Sherry (which is sometimes sweetened after fermentation and in England once bore the nickname of "sack"); another theory is that the term derived from the Japanese drink sake, being introduced by Spanish and Portuguese traders.
- **Short mead** — Also called "quick mead." A type of mead recipe that is meant to age quickly, for immediate consumption. Because of the techniques used in its creation, short mead shares some qualities found in cider (or even light ale): primarily that it is effervescent, and often has a cidery taste.[citation needed] It can also be champagne-like.
- **Show mead** — A term which has come to mean "plain" mead: that which has honey and water as a base, with no fruits, spices or extra flavorings. Since honey alone often does not provide enough nourishment for the yeast to carry on its lifecycle, a mead that is devoid of fruit, etc. will sometimes require a special yeast nutrient and other enzymes to produce an acceptable finished product. In most competitions including all those using the BJCP style guidelines as well as the International Mead Fest, the term "traditional mead" is used for this

variety. It should be considered, however, that since mead is historically a very variable product, such recent (and artificial) guidelines apply mainly to competition judging as a means of providing a common language; style guidelines, per se, do not really apply to commercial and historical examples of this or any type of mead.

- **Sima** - a quickly fermented low-alcoholic Finnish variety, seasoned with lemon and associated with the festival of vappu.
- **Tej** — Tej is an Ethiopian mead, fermented with wild yeasts (and bacteria), and with the addition of gesho. Recipes vary from family to family, with some recipes leaning towards braggot with the inclusion of grains.
- **Trójniak** — A Polish mead, made using two units of water for each unit of honey.
- **White mead** — A mead that is colored white, either from herbs or fruit used or sometimes egg whites.

Making Mead at Home[21]

"This document is a list of basic information about mead and mead making for the beginner. It is intended to get you started and answer your initial questions about mead and mead making.

What Kinds of Honey?

There are many kinds of honey, based on which flowers the bees collected the nectar from. Bees aren't loyal to any particular flower, so any characterization of honey as being from a particular source (for example, "blackberry honey") can vary from absolutely true, to a rough generality, depending on what flowers the bees can find and how interesting they find them. Honeys range in taste and color from the light clover through alfalfa to stronger tasting (and darker) such as buckwheat. There are many unusual honeys to be found where there are unusual local flowers. Which honey you will use depends both on which you like the taste of, and what type of mead you are trying to make. Stronger flavors go well in metheglins

---

[21] By John Dilley, Dick Dunn, Thomas Manteufel, and Michael Tighe.

and heavier or sweet meads, while the milder honeys make a good base for melomels or dry traditional meads.

You can buy honey in bulk from roadside stands or health food stores. You may be lucky enough to live near an apiary and be able to buy right from the beekeeper. Look in the phone book for honey, health food, or beekeepers. Sometimes, exterminators will remove hives, give the bees to beekeepers, and sell the honey. University agriculture departments occasionally sell honey. Be inventive. If all else fails, you may have to buy it from the grocery store.

The honey will be either raw or processed in some way. Raw honey has bits of wax, bee parts, dust, pollen, microorganisms, and the like in it. You have the most control in how you process raw honey, but you also have the most to do. Honey may be filtered, or blended, or even heat pasteurized to make it clearer and less likely to crystallize. The more processed it is, the milder it is likely to be and the less character it will give to your mead. Processing also evaporates some of the honey's aroma. Commercial, grocery store honey is the most processed and is generally not a good choice for mead making.

Crystallized honey is just fine for mead. In fact, it has two points in its favor: First, it generally indicates less processing, since one of the reasons for processing honey is to keep it from crystallizing. Second, it may be cheaper because it's less appealing to the average consumer. To re- liquefy crystallized honey so you can pour it, just heat it gently.

Adding Acid

Acid is added to the **"must"** (the honey water mixture you're going to ferment) both to adjust the ph and to balance the sweet flavor of the honey. Yeast love an acidic environment. Many other micro-organisms don't. The acid you add protects the must until the alcohol level creates a hostile environment for the competition.

Acid can be added in many forms. Winemaking suppliers sell acid blends, powder or liquid. Acid is measured in "as tartaric", or how acidic the must is compared to pure tartaric acid. For example, if the must is 0.5 percent acid as tartaric, it is as acidic as if 0.5 percent of the must were pure tartaric acid. Inexpensive test kits will let you measure the acidity so that you can adjust it. Acid blends are a combination of tartaric, citric, and malic acids. You may be able to get the individual acids used in blends. Each contributes a slightly different taste in addition to acidity. The natural acid in fruits and berries will also acidify the must, for which reason melomels often need no additional acid.

How to Prepare the "Must"

The honey/water before fermenting is called must. You will want to add the honey to hot water in a large pot, but make sure the pot is not on the heat while doing this because the honey will fall to the bottom and caramelize (or stir vigorously if you leave it on the heat). Stainless steel or enameled kettles are preferred.

Some mead recipes recommend only heating the must enough to pasteurize it. This is because boiling mead will drive off some of the delicate honey flavors.

If scum rises while heating or boiling the must, skim it off. It consists of wax, bee parts, pollen, etc., which don't help the flavor of the mead.

An alternative preparation method involves the use of "Campden tablets" or "sulfiting" to sterilize the must. If you're a winemaker, you'll recognize this method. With the use of Campden tablets, it is not necessary to heat/ boil the must at all first, although some mead-makers do so anyway for the sake of clarity of the final mead. If you use Campden tablets, follow a recipe or instructions for quantity, preparation, delay times, etc. Heating is probably easier than sulfiting for the beginning mead-maker.

Yeasts

Mead is more a wine than beer, with a final alcohol level anywhere between 10 and 18 percent. Wine yeasts, which have a higher alcohol tolerance, may ferment slower at first (although some are remarkably fast) but will ferment more completely than ale or lager yeast. They are also less likely to produce "off" tastes which take a long time to age out after the mead is finished. A partial list of some of the popular yeasts are: Champagne (multiple strains), Epernay, Flor Sherry, Steinberg, Prise De Mousse, Tokay, and various proprietary strains which are derived from these.

Figure 63 - Mead from the Sticky Mouth Honey Company

This list is by no means exhaustive. Each yeast will impart its own unique characteristic to the mead. Champagne ferments out very dry and has a high alcohol tolerance. Epernay has a fruity bouquet. Flor Sherry has a high alcohol tolerance and contributes a flavor that goes better with sack meads. Prise de Mousse is particularly neutral and fast-fermenting. Some yeasts will produce noticeable levels of phenols (the throat-burning part of cough medicine), which age out eventually in bottle conditioning but are an un- necessary complication since there are yeasts that don't produce them.

Yeast Nutrient

Honey by itself is low in some of the nutrients that yeast need to reproduce and quickly ferment out the mead must. Fermentation times can be measured in months as the yeast slowly trickles along. This is a disadvantage because as long as the fermenting mead remains sweet and low in alcohol, it is inviting to contaminating bacteria. Mead makers can add a nutrient to help the yeast, and normally should do so if the only fermentable ingredient is honey. Fruit, particularly grapes, will contribute needed ingredients; thus melomels have lesser or no requirement for nutrients. Nutrients are normally added when the must is prepared.

There are several kinds of nutrients. Most winemaking shops will sell various salts designed for grape musts. While this is helpful for mead, too much can leave an astringent metallic flavor that will take months or years in the bottle to age out. Yeast extract, pulverized yeast, is also available. Dead yeast are exploded ultrasonically or in a centrifuge, and sold as a powder. Yeast extract will not leave the same metallic flavors as nutrients, but may be more difficult to find. It is not possible to make your own yeast extract at home.

Fermentation

Mead will take longer than beer to ferment. Fermentation times can be measured in months, so get another carboy. Mead likes to ferment a little warmer than beer (70F - 80F), but should be stored in a cool place to bottle condition. You will have to rack mead (transfer it to a separate vessel, leaving behind the sediment) while it is

Figure 64 - Carboy with Gas Lock

fermenting. If you make any kind of mead beside traditional, you will have to rack about a week after starting to remove the bits of fruit and spices that settle out. Rack periodically after that to get the mead off the dead yeast and other matter that settles out--every 3-6 weeks depending on the rate of fermentation and settling. This improves the flavor and clarifies the mead.

Initial fermentation of melomels made with fruit (not just juice) is easiest in a food-grade plastic pail so that you can strain out the fruit before racking. Except for this, glass carboys with fermentation locks are the best fermentation vessels.

Bottling

First, you must make sure the mead has stopped fermenting. Mead is so slow to ferment that it may appear completely done, yet continue to ferment after bottling. This can turn a still mead into a sparkling one; it can even produce enough pressure to cause the bottles to explode. Exploding bottles-- "glass grenades"--aren't funny. They're unpredictable and very dangerous.

To be sure the mead is done fermenting, take hydrometer readings spanning a week or more and be sure the readings are not still falling. Dry meads will also finish at a gravity below 1.000. As a mead finishes, it will "fall clear"--the initial cloudiness will settle out. Be careful, though, because being clear is not enough.

Figure 65 - Hydrometer

Choose appropriate bottles for the type of mead. Sparkling mead (carbonated, like champagne) will require a sturdy bottle, either sparkling wine (which are thick enough to take the higher carbonation) or returnable beer bottles. Beer bottles should be crown-capped. Sparkling wine bottles can be corked if you use champagne corks and wire them down. American sparkling-wine bottles can be crown-capped just as beer bottles can. European sparkling-wine bottles cannot be reliably crown-capped--they have a crown-cap lip, but it's the wrong size for standard caps.

Still meads (noncarbonated, like normal wines) may be bottled in regular wine bottles with standard corks, or in crown-capped bottles as above. Since pressure isn't an issue, almost any bottle with an airtight closure can be made to work. Bear in mind, though, that the appearance of your bottles is part of the first impression when you serve your mead.

Mead that has finished fermentation and is then bottled will be "still" (flat). Sparkling mead is "primed" by adding a small amount of sugar at bottling time to produce a short renewed fermentation so that it is carbonated. For predictable results (again, to avoid "glass grenades"), you should first let the mead finish fermenting in the carboy, then add just the amount of sugar needed to carbonate it. Bottling a mead before it finished fermenting (in hopes of capturing just the right amount of carbonation in the bottle) can lead to under- or over-carbonation, and even in the best case won't give the mead a chance to finish clearing before bottling. A normal amount of priming sugar is about 4 ounces by weight for five gallons.

Store the bottles in a cool dark place. Mead is not as sensitive as beer to light (unless you have hops in it), but should not be left in bright light.

Legality

In the USA, mead is classified as a wine. A brief, informal (not legal advice!) synopsis: Federal regulations allow an adult to make up to 100 gallons a year, or 200 gallons per year per household of two or more adults, for personal or family use, with no tax or license required. It may not be sold. Concentration (including but not limited to distillation) is prohibited. State and local laws may impose additional restrictions, so check first. The usual situation is that home mead-making is allowed in any locality where commercial wine can be sold. Repeat: this is NOT legal advice."

Northern Cookbook

Now that we've whet our apetites with talk of mead, lets move on to a scrumptious collection of old recipes.

Please enjoy the following Medieval, Anglo Saxon & Viking Recipes.

Figure 66 - Viking Era Style Kitchen

A

Jellie of Fyshe

Ingredients – Serves 6

- 225 g (8 oz) hake, cod, haddock, or other well-flavored white fish
- 3 scallops
- 75 g (3 oz) prawns (shrimp)
- 2 onions, roughly sliced
- 1 tablespoon white wine vinegar
- 25g (1 oz) ginger root, peeled and finely chopped
- 1/3 teaspoon sea salt, 1/4 teaspoon white pepper
- 450mL (15 fl oz, 2 cups) each white wine and water
- 20g (3/4 oz) gelatine

Method

1. Put the white fish in a pan with the onions, vinegar, ginger root, spices, wine and water.
2. Bring it gently to the boil and simmer for 10 minutes.
3. Add the scallops and prawns and cook for a further 3 minutes.
4. Remove the fish; bone and skin the white fish and set it all aside.
5. Strain the cooking juices and set aside to cool for several hours by which time a lot of the sediment will have settled in the bottom of the bowl. Carefully pour off the juices, leaving the sediment, and then strain several times through a clean tea cloth. You should have approximately 750mL (25 fl oz, 3 cups) of liquid left. Melt 20g (3/4 oz) of gelatin in a little of the liquid, cool it to room temperature, then mix it into the rest of the juices.
6. Pour a thin layer 1 cm (1/2 inch) of the juice into the bottom of a 1.2 liter (2 pint, 5 cup) soufflé dish or fish mold and put it in the fridge to set.
7. Flake the white fish into smallish flakes; remove the coral from the scallops and cut the white flesh into three of four pieces.

8. Once the jelly is firm, arrange the most decorative of the fish in the bottom of the dish-- some scallop coral in the middle, prawns around the outsides, flakes of white fish in between or however you feel inspired.

9. Spoon a little more of the juice and return it to the fridge to set.

10. Continue to layer the fish in the mould, setting each layer with a covering of juice until you have used up all the fish and juices.

11. Leave the jelly to set for at least 4 hours in a fridge.

12. Unmold and decorate with fresh herbs;

13. Serve as a starter.

Crustade of Chicken and Pigeon

Ingredients – Serves 6

- 225-350g (8-12oz) wholemeal or wholewheat pastry (depending on whether you want a lid on your crustade)
- 1 pigeon
- 2 chicken joints (2 breasts or 2 whole legs)
- 150mL (f fl oz, 2/3 cup) dry white wine
- several grinds of black pepper
- 4 cloves
- 15 g (1/2 oz) butter
- 50g (2oz) mushrooms, roughly chopped
- 25g (1oz) raisins
- 3 large eggs
- salt, pepper, and 1/2 teaspoon ground ginger

Method

1. Roll out 225g (8 oz) of the pastry and line a 20cm (8 inch) flan dish; back the crust blind.

2. Put the pigeon in a pot with the stock, wine, pepper and cloves and cook very slowly for an hour.

3. Add the chicken and continue to cook for a further 45 minutes or till the meat of both birds is really tender.

173

4. Meanwhile cook the mushrooms lightly in the butter.

5. Remove the birds from the stock and bone them. Cut the flesh into quite small pieces, mix it with the mushrooms and the raisins and spread them over the base of the flan case.

6. Beat the eggs with a fork and season with the salt, pepper, and ginger

7. Add 240mL (8floz, 1 cup) of the cooking juices and pour over the meat in the flan case. If you want to have a lid, roll out the rest of the pastry and cover the flan.

8. Bake it in moderate oven (180C, 350F, Gas Mark4) for 25 minutes if uncovered, 35 minutes if covered. Serve warm with a good green salad.

For a more 20th century flavor - double the chicken, leave out the pigeon, and substitute 25g (1 oz) chopped fried bacon for the raisins.

Fenkel in Soppes' or Braised Fennel with Ginger

The original version of this recipe comes from the "Forme of Cury," a collection of 196 "receipts" copied by Richard II's scribes at his cooks' directions.

Ingredients – Serves 6

- 750g (1 1/2 lb) trimmed, fresh fennel root; cleaned and cut in matchsticks
- 225g (8 oz) onions, thickly sliced
- 1 heaped teaspoon of ground ginger
- 1 level teapsoon of powdered saffron
- 1/2 teaspoon of salt
- 2 tablespoon olive oil
- 150mL (5 fl oz, 2/3 cup) each dry white wine and water
- 6 thick slices of coarse wholewheat or wholemeal bread (optional)

Method

1. Put the fennel in a wide, lidded pan with the onions.

2. Sprinkle over the spices and salt, then the oil and finally pour over the liquids.

3. Bring to the boil, cover and simmer for 20-30 minutes or till the fennel is cooked without being mushy.

4. Stir once or twice during the cooking to make sure the spices get well distributed.

5. Serve it alone with a roast meat or griddled fish or place one slice of bread on each warmed plate, cover it with the fennel and pour over the juices.

Lozenges or Curd Cheese Pastries

Ingredients – Serves 6

- 225g (8oz) wholemeal or wholewheat shortcrust pastry
- 225g (8 oz) curd cheese
- 25g (1oz) very finely chopped stem or crystallized ginger or plump raisins
- 15g (1/2 oz) toasted and chopped pine nuts
- sugar to taste
- lemon juice to taste

Method

1. Roll the pastry out very thin and cut it into small rectangles-- approximately 15x8 cm (6x3 inches). You should have at least 24.
2. Bake them in a moderately hot oven (190C, 375F, Gas Mark 5) for ten minutes or till they are crisp and brown.
3. Remove them and cool on a rack.
4. Meanwhile mix the curd cheese with the ginger or raisins, the pine nuts and the sugar and lemon to taste.
5. Set aside.
6. When you are ready to serve, sandwich together two pieces of pastry with the cheese mixture.
7. They can be used as a dessert or as a snack.

Griddled Trout With Herbs

The herbs below are what might have been used in Anglo-Saxon East Anglia, but use whatever you might fancy. Try to use fresh, although dried is acceptable.

Ingredients – Serves 6

- 6 fresh cleaned trout
- 6 sprigs fresh rosemary, or 1-2 tablespoons dried
- 75g (3 oz) soft butter
- 18 fresh mint leaves or 2 teaspoons dried
- leaves from 6 sprigs fresh thyme or 2 teaspoons dried
- 6 fresh sage leaves or 1 scant teaspoon dried
- 1-2 teaspoons coarse sea salt
- 6-9 grinds black pepper

Method

1. Put one sprig or generous shake of rosemary down the middle of each fish.
2. Chop all the other herbs and seasonings and mash them into the soft butter.
3. Use this to coat the fish generously on each side.
4. Griddle, barbeque or grill it for 4-5 minutes on each side or till the skin is well browned and the flesh flaking off the bone.
5. Baste now and then with the butter which runs off.
6. Serve at once with lot of fresh bread and a salad or a simple green vegetable.

Hare, Rabbit, Veal or Chicken Stew with Herbs & Barley

In 7th century England, herbs were one of the few flavourings available to cooks and were used heavily.

Ingredients – Serves 6

- 50g (2oz) butter
- 1 -1.5kg (2-3 lb) (depending on the amount of bone) of hare or rabbit
- joints, stewing veal or chicken joints
- 450g (1lb) washed and trimmed leeks, thickly sliced
- 4 cloves garlic, chopped finely
- 175 g (6 oz) pot barley
- 900 mL (30 fl oz, 3 3/4 cups) water
- 3 generous tablespoons red or white wine vinegar
- 2 bay leaves, salt, pepper
- 15 fresh, roughly chopped sage leaves, or 1 tablespoon dried sage

Method

1. Melt the butter in a heavy pan and fry the meat with the leeks and garlic till the vegetables are slightly softened and the meat lightly browned.
2. Add the barley, water, vinegar, bay leaves and seasoning.
3. Bring the pot to the boil, cover it and simmer gently for 1 - 1 1/2 hours or till the meat is really tender and ready to fall from the bone.
4. Add the sage and continue to cook for several minutes.
5. Adjust the seasoning to taste and serve in bowls-- the barley will serve as a vegetable.

Small Bird and Bacon Stew with Walnuts or Hazelnuts

Ingredients – Serves 6

- 6 fatty rashers of bacon, chopped roughly
- 3 cloves garlic
- 4 pigeons or other small game birds (6 if very small)
- 225 g (8 oz) mushrooms, whatever variety, chopped roughly
- 75 g (3 oz) roughly chopped roasted hazelnuts or walnuts
- 300 ml (10 fl oz, 1 1/4 cups) real ale
- 150 ml (5 fl oz, 3/4 cup) water
- 2 or 3 bay leaves
- a little salt and freshly ground black pepper
- 6 coarse slices brown bread

Method

1. Fry the bacon, with the garlic, till it is lightly browned in a heavy bottomed casserole.
2. Add birds and brown on all sides.
3. Add the mushrooms and nuts, continue to cook for a couple of minutes, then add the ale and water with the bay leaves.
4. Bring to the boil, cover and simmer very gently for 2 - 2 1/2 hours - the birds should be falling off the bone.
5. Remove the birds from the juices, cool juices completely and remove any excess fat.
6. The birds can be served whole on or off the bone. If the latter, carve them while they are cold then return to the skimmed juices and reheat gently.
7. Adjust the seasoning to taste and serve either the whole birds of the slices on the pieces of bread, with plenty of the juices and "bits".
8. A good green salad to follow is the best accompaniment.

Summer Fruit, Honey, and Hazelnut Crumble

....A baked dessert like this would have been sunk in the embers of the log fire with a cauldron or pot upturned over it to form a lid...

Ingredients – Serves 6

- 1 kg (2 1/2 lb) mixed soft summer fruits-- raspberries, loganberries,
- strawberries, currants, bilberries or whatever is available
- honey or brown sugar to taste
- 75 g (3 oz) tasted hazelnuts
- 75 g (3 oz) wholemeal or wholewheat brown breadcrumbs

Method

1. Put the fruits in a pan or microwave dish with about 20 cm (1 inch) water in the bottom and cook gently for 10-15 minutes (4-6 minutes in microwave), or till the fruits are soft without being totally mushy.
2. Sweeten to taste with honey or brown sugar (Saxons would have used honey); how much you need will depend on what fruits you have used.
3. Drain the excess juice and save to serve with the pudding.
4. Chop the hazelnuts in a processor or liquidiser until they are almost as fine as the breadcrumbs, but not quite, then mix the two together.
5. Spoon the fruit into an ovenproof dish and cover with a thick layer of hazelnuts and crumbs.
6. Bake in a moderate oven (180C, 350F, Gas Mark 4) for 20 – 30 minutes or till the top is slightly crunchy and browned.
7. Serve with lots of cream or plain yogurt and the warmed fruit juices.

Honey Oat Cakes

These are easy to make and very tasty.

Ingredients – Serves 10–15

- 350 g (12 Oz) Rolled Oats (Whole rolled oats if possible)
- 225 g (8 Oz) Butter
- 225 g (8 Oz) Honey
- Pinch of salt

Method

1. Melt the butter in a medium sized saucepan. Add the salt, honey and oats and stir until they are well mixed.
2. Spoon the mixture out onto a greased baking tray or swiss roll tin and press it down well.
3. Bake at 325F/170C for 30 minutes or until golden brown.
4. Cool for a few minutes then mark into squares while still warm and serve when cold.

Part 3
Spirit of the North

In **Part 3**, we'll look at the "Spirit of the North", or **esoteric** [22]knowledge. How did the world begin according to our folk? Who created us? Who did they pay homage to in times of need? We'll also explore the use of the runes for divination , meditation and magic.

We'll talk allot about "Norse" lore, but this lore was similar in many respects across North West Europe. The Poetic Edda, Prose Edda, and Icelandic Sagas are our primary written sources for much of the mythological lore, hence the Norse focus.

---

[22] Esoteric knowledge is that which is available only to a narrow circle of "enlightened", "initiated", or specially educated people.

Faith… Must be enforced by reason…When faith becomes blind it dies.
- Mahatma Gandhi

Chapter 7 – Northern Mythology

Creation

orthern mythology is grand and tragic. Its principal theme is the perpetual struggle of the beneficent forces of Nature against the injurious, and hence it is not graceful and idyllic in character like the religion of the sunny South, where the people could bask in perpetual sunshine, and the fruits of the earth grew ready to their hand.

It was very natural that the dangers incurred in hunting and fishing under these inclement skies, and the suffering entailed by the long cold winters when the sun never shines, made our ancestors contemplate cold and ice as malevolent spirits; and it was with equal reason that they invoked with special fervor the beneficent influences of heat and light.

When questioned Concerning the creation of the world, the Northern skalds or poets, who's songs are preserved in the Eddas and Sagas, declared that in the beginning, when darkness rested over all,

Figure 67 - Creation as depicted on a Faroe Islands postage stamp (2003) by Anker Eli Petersen.

there existed a powerful being called Allfather, whom they dimly conceived as uncreated as well as unseen, and that whatever he willed came to pass.[23]

In Thorpe's *Northern Mythology*, we are told that in the beginning of time a world existed in the north called **Niflheim**, in the middle of which was a well called **Hvergelmir**, from which flowed twelve rivers[24]. In the south part there was another world, **Muspellheim**[25], a light and hot, a flaming and radiant world, the boundary of which was guarded by **Surt** with a flaming sword. Cold and heat contended with each other. From Niflheim flowed the poisonous cold streams called **Elivagar**[26] (*Ice Waves*), which became hardened into ice, so that one layer of ice was piled on another in **Ginnunga-gap**, or the abyss of abysses, which faced the north; but from the south issued heat from Muspellheim, and the sparks glittered so that the south part of Ginnunga-gap was as light as the purest air. The heat met the ice, which melted and dripped; the drops then, through his power who sent forth the heat, received life, and a human form was produced called **Ymir**[27], the progenitor of the Frost-giants (Hrimjmrsar), who by the Frost-giants is also called **Aurgelmir**, that is, the ancient mass or chaos. He was not a god, but was evil, together with all his race. As yet there was neither sand nor sea nor cool waves, neither earth nor grass nor vaulted heaven, but only Ginnunga-gap, the abyss of abysses. Ymir was nourished from four streams of milk, which flowed from the udder of the cow **Audhumla**, a being that came into existence by the power of Surt.

---

[23] Much of this chapter comes directly from *Myths of Northern Lands* by H.A. Guerber

[24] Their names are Sval, Gunnthra, Fiorm, Fimbul, Thul, Slid, Hrid, Sylg, Ylg, Vid, Leipt, Gioll, which last is nearest to the barred gates of Hel.

[25] The word Muspell has disappeared from all the Germanic tongues, except the Old-Saxon and the Old High German, where it signifies fire at the destruction of the world.

[26] From el, a storm, and vagr (pi. vagar), river, wave. From el, *a storm,* and vagr (pi. vagar), *river, wave.*

[27] Ym from ymia, *to make a noise, rush, roar.* He who sent forth the heat is not Surt, who is only the guardian of Muspellheim, but a supreme ineffable being.

From Ymir there came forth offspring while he slept: for having fallen into a sweat, from under his left arm there grew a man and a woman, and one of his feet begat a son by the other. At this time, before heaven and earth existed, the Universal Father (Alfathr) was among the Hrimthursar, or Frost-giants.

The cow Audhumla licked the frost-covered stones that were salt, and the first day, towards evening, there came forth from them a man's hair, the second day a head, the third day an entire man. He was called **Buri** (the producing) ; he was comely of countenance, tall and powerful. His son, **Bor** (the produced), was married to **Bestla**, a daughter of the giant **Bolthorn**, and they had three sons, **Odin**, **Vili** and **Ve**. These brothers were gods, and created heaven and earth.

Bor's sons slew the giant Ymir, and there ran so much blood from his wound that all the frost-giants were drowned in it, except the giant **Bergelmir** (whose father was Thrudgelmir, and whose grandfather was Aurgelmir), who escaped with his wife on a chest, and continued the race of the frost-giants. But Bor's sons carried the body of Ymir into the middle of Ginnunga-gap, and formed of it the earth, of his blood the seas and waters, of his bones the mountains, of his teeth and grinders and those bones that were broken, they made stones and pebbles; from the blood that flowed from his wounds they made the great impassable ocean, in which they fixed the earth, around which it lies in a circle; of his skull they formed the heaven, and set it up over the earth with four regions, and under each corner placed a dwarf, the names of whom were **Austri**, **Vestri**, **Northri**, **Suthri**; of his brain they formed the heavy clouds, of his hair the vegetable creation, and of his eyebrows a wall of defense against the giants round **Midgard**, the middlemost part of the earth, the dwelling-place of the sons of men. They then took the sparks and glowing cinders that were cast out of Muspellheim, and set them in heaven, both above and below, to illumine heaven and earth. They also assigned places for the lightning and fiery meteors, some in heaven, and some unconfined under heaven, and appointed to them a course. Hence, " as it is said in old philosophy," arose the division of years and days. Thus Bor's sons raised up the heavenly disks, and the sun shone on the cold stones, so that the earth was decked with green herbs. The sun from the south followed the moon, and cast her[28] right arm round the heavenly horses' door (the east) ; but she knew not where her dwelling lay, the moon knew not his power, nor did the stars know where they had a station. Then the holy gods consulted together, and gave to every light its place, and a name to the new moon (Nyi), and to the waning moon (Nithi), and gave names to the morning and the mid-day, to the forenoon and the evening, that the children of men, sons of time, might reckon the years thereafter.

Night (**Nott**) and Day (**Dagr**) were of opposite races. Night, of giant race, was dark, like her father, the giant Norvi (or Narfi). She was first married to Naglfari, and had by him a son named Aud;

secondly to Anar (or Onar); their daughter was Earth (Jorth); lastly to Delling, and their son was Day, who was fair, bright and beautiful, through his paternal descent. All-father took Night and Day, and gave them two horses and two cars, and placed them in heaven, that they might ride successively, in twenty-four hours' time, round the earth. Night rides

Figure 68 - Nótt rides her horse in this 19th century painting by Peter Nicolai Arbo.

first with her horse which is named **Hrimfaxi**, that bedews the earth each morn with the

[28] In Northern tradition the sun is female, and the moon male

drops from his bit. He is also called Fiorsvartnir.

The horse belonging to Day is called **Skinfaxi**, from whose shining mane light beams forth over heaven and earth. He is also called Glad (Gladr) and Drosul. The Moon and the Sun are brother and sister; they are the children of Mundilfari, who, on account of their beauty, called his son **Mani**, and his daughter **Sol** (or **Sunna**); for which presumption the gods in their anger took brother and sister and placed them in heaven, and appointed Sol to drive the horses that draw the chariot of

Figure 69 - "Dagr" (1874) by Peter Nicolai Arbo.

the sun, which the gods had formed, to give light to the world, of the sparks from Muspellheim. Sol was married to a man named Glen (Glenur, Glanur), and has to her car the horses **Arvakur** (the watchful), and **Alsvith** (the rapid), under whose shoulders the gods placed an ice-cold breeze to cool them. **Svalin** (the cooling) is the name of a shield that stands before the sun, which would else set waves and mountains on fire. Mani directs the course of the moon, and regulates Nyi and Nithi. He once took up two children from the earth, Bil and Hiuki (Hviki), as they were going from the well of Byrgir, bearing on their shoulders the bucket Saeg, and the pole Simul. Their father was Vidfinn; they follow Mani, as may be observed from the earth. There are also two wolves to be mentioned, one of which, named **Skoll**, follows the sun, and which she fears will swallow her; the other called **Hati**, the son of Hrodvitnir, runs before the sun, and strives to seize on the moon, and so in the end it will be.

The mother of these wolves is a giantess, who dwells in a wood to the east of Midgard, called Jarnvid (Jarnviftr), in which those female demons (trollkonur) dwell called Jarnvids (JarnvrSjur). She brought forth many sons, who are giants, and all in the form of wolves. One of this race, named **Managarm** (or **Garm**), is said to be the most powerful; he will be sated with the lives of all dying persons; he will swallow up the moon, and thereby besprinkle both heaven and air with blood.

Then will the sun lose its brightness, and the winds rage and howl in all directions, as it is said:

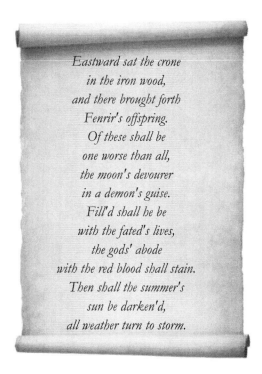

Eastward sat the crone
in the iron wood,
and there brought forth
Fenrir's offspring.
Of these shall be
one worse than all,
the moon's devourer
in a demon's guise.
Fill'd shall he be
with the fated's lives,
the gods' abode
with the red blood shall stain.
Then shall the summer's
sun be darken'd,
all weather turn to storm.

Figure 70 - "The Wolves Pursuing Sol and Mani" (1909) by J. C. Dollman.

The father of Winter (Vetur) was called Vindsval, of Summer (Sumar), Svasud (Svasuftr). Both shall reign every year until the gods pass away. At the end of heaven sits the giant Hraesvelg, in an eagle's garb. From the motion of his wings comes the wind which passes over men

Thus the first created beings were Ymir and his race, the giants; next were the gods, who created heaven and earth; not until these were in existence, and ready as places of abode for living beings, were the dwarfs and human race created[29].

The mighty gods, or Aesir, assembled on Ida's plain (Idavoll) in the middle of their city Asgard. There they first erected a court (hof), wherein were seats for all the twelve, and a high seat for All-father; also a lofty burgh or hall (havrgr) for the goddesses, called Vingolf.

---

[29] Both giants and dwarfs shun the light. If surprised by the breaking forth of day, they become changed to stone. In the Alvismal, Thor amuses the dwarf Alvis with various questions till daylight, and then coolly says to him, " With great artifices, I tell thee, thou hast been deceived ; thou art surprised here, dwarf! by daylight: the sun now shines in the hall."

They then constructed a smithy, made hammers, tongs, anvils and, in time, all other requisite implements. There they worked in metal, stone and wood, and so extensively in the metal called gold, that all their household gear was formed of it, whence that age was called the Golden Age. This lasted until it was corrupted by the women that came from Jotunheim.

Figure 71 - Ask and Embla as depicted on a Faroe Islands postage stamp (2003) by Anker Eli Petersen.

Then the gods sitting on their thrones held counsel. They considered how the dwarfs had been quickened in the mould down in the earth, like maggots in a dead body:

for the dwarfs had been first created[30], and received life in the carcass of Ymir, and were then maggots; but now, by the decree of the gods, they received human understanding and human bodies, though they dwell in the earth and in stones. Modsognir was the chief, the second Durin. The dwarfs of Lofar's race betook themselves from the Rocky Hall (Salar-Steinn) over the earth-field's regions (Aurvangur) to Jora's plains (Joruvellir).

Their several names bear allusion to the subordinate powers of nature in the mineral and vegetable kingdoms, and express the operating power which penetrates the soil, the veins of stone, the sap of plants; also the cold and heat, the light and the colors which are thereby produced.

Men came into existence when three mighty, benevolent gods, Odin, Hoenir and Lodur, left the assembly to make an excursion. On the earth they found **Ask** and **Embla** (ash and elm),

---

[30] According to Snorri's Edda the dwarfs were created after mankind, while in the other Edda it is the reverse.

with little power and without destiny: spirit they had not, nor sense, nor blood, nor power of motion, nor fair color. Odin gave them spirit (breath), Hoenir sense, Lodur blood and fair color.

In Snorri's Edda it's told that Bor's sons (Odin, Vili and Ve) walking on the sea-shore found two trees, which they took up, and created men of them. The first gave them spirit and life; the second, understanding and power of motion; the third, aspect, speech, hearing and sight. The man they called Ask, the woman Embla. From this pair the whole human race is descended, to whom a dwelling was assigned in Midgard.

Cosmology

In Norse mythology, there are nine worlds, unified by the world tree Yggdrasil:

- **Asgard**, world of the Aesir.
- **Ljossálfaheim**, world of the Light Álfar (elves).
- **Vanaheim**, world of the Vanir.
- **Midgard**, world of humans (Middle Garden).
- **Niflheim**, world of the primordial element of ice.
- **Muspellheim**, world of the primordial element of fire.
- **Jotunheim**, world of the jötnar (Giants).
- **Svartálfaheim**, world of the Svartálfar (dark elves or dwarves)
- **Helheim**, underground world of the dead.

The Norse creation myth tells how everything came into existence and how the world of men was created by the gods. Mapping the nine worlds however, escapes precision because the Poetic Edda often alludes vaguely, and the Prose Edda may be influenced by medieval Christian cosmology. The following is from Thorpe's *Northern Mythology*:

The earth is flat and round; about it is the deep ocean. Outermost of all, around the shore, is the giants' abode, Jotunheim or Utgard, against whose attacks the gods raised a bulwark within, around Midgard, formed of Ymir's eyebrows. In the middle of the world, and on the highest spot, dwell Aesir in **Asgard**, where All-father Odin established rulers, who with himself should preside over the burgh and the destinies of men. There is the largest and noblest of all dwellings, **Gladsheim**, and another, roofed with silver, called **Valaskialf**, which Odin, in the beginning of time, curiously constructed, and from the throne in which (**Hlidskialf**) he looks out over all worlds, and learns the doings of all creatures.

At the world's southern end there is a hall, the fairest of all and brighter than the sun, which is called **Gimli**. That will stand when both heaven and earth are past away, and good and upright men will inhabit that place to all eternity. It is, moreover, said that there is another heaven to the south, above this, which is called **Andlang**, and a third still higher called **Vidblain**, in which last we believe this hall to be; but we believe that only the Light Elves now inhabit those places.

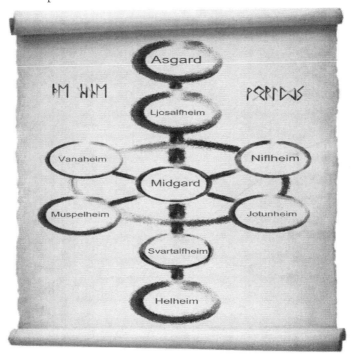

Figure 72 - The 9 Worlds

In another hall, as we have already seen, is the abode of the goddesses, which men call **Vingolf**. Between the giants and the gods flows the river Ifing, on which ice never comes.

From Midgard to Asgard leads the bridge **Bifrost** (the quaking space), known to mortals as the rainbow: it has three colors.

The most sacred place or seat of the gods is by the ash

Yggdrasil, where they daily sit in judgment. Yggdrasil is the largest and best of trees; its branches spread themselves over the whole world, and tower up above the heavens. It has three roots which reach far and wide. Under one of them is the abode of Hel, the goddess of the dead; under the second dwell the frost giants ; under the third, human beings. Or,

Figure 73 - The god Heimdallr stands before the rainbow bridge while blowing a horn (1905) by Emil Doepler.

according to the prose Edda, the first root reaches to the Aesir; the second to the frost-giants, where was formerly Ginnunga-gap, while the third stands over Niflheim, under which is Hvergelmir. This root is constantly gnawed from beneath by the serpent Nidhogg. Under the second root is Mimir's well, in which wisdom and genius are concealed. Mimir, the owner of the well, is full of wisdom, because he drinks every morning of the well from the horn Gioll (Giallar-horn). All-father once came, and craved a draught from the well, but got it not before he had given an eye as a pledge; whence it is said that Mimir drinks mead every morning from Valfather's pledge. Under the root which reaches to the Aesir's abode, is the sacred fountain of Urd, where the gods sit in judgment. Every day the Aesir ride thither over Bifrost, which is likewise called the Aesir-bridge (Asbni). The names of the Aesir's horses are as follow: **Sleipnir**, which is the best, and belongs to Odin, has eight legs, Glad, Gyllir,

Gler, Skeidbrimir, Silfrintop, Sinir, Gils, Falhofnir, Gulltop, Lettfeti. Baldur's horse was burnt with him, and Thor walks to the meeting, and wades through the rivers Kormt and Ormt, and the two Kerlaugs, else the Aesir's bridge would be in a blaze, and the sacred water boil.

By the well of Urd there stands, under the ash-tree, a fair hall, from which go three maidens, Urd, Verdandi, and Skuld (past time, present time, and future time). They are called Norns (Nornir); they

grave on the tablet (shield), determine the life, and fix the destiny of the children of men. But besides these there are other Norns, those that are present at the birth of every child, to determine its destiny.

These are of the race of the gods, while some others are of elf-race, and others of the dwarf-kin, or daughters of Dvalin. The good Norns and those of good descent allot good fortune; and when men fall into misfortunes, it is to be ascribed to the evil Norns. Mention occurs of the dogs of the Norns.

Figure 74 - The Norns under Yggdrasil as depicted on a Faroe Islands postage stamp (2003) by Anker Eli Petersen.

In the branches of the tree Yggdrasil sits an eagle that knows many things. Between his eyes sits the hawk **Vedurfolnir**. The squirrel **Ratatosk** runs up and down the tree, and bears rancorous words between the eagle and the serpent Nidhogg. Four harts run among the boughs and bite its buds; their names are, **Dain, Dvalin, Dunneyr** and **Durathror**.

Those Norns that dwell by the well of Urd take water every day from the spring, which, with the mud that lies about it, they pour over the ash, that its branches may not rot and perish. This water is so sacred, that everything that enters it becomes as white as the film of an egg-shell, as it is said in the Voluspa.

The dew that falls from its branches on the earth is by men called honey-dew, and is the food of bees. Two birds are fed in the well of Urd, called swans, and from them descend the birds of that species.

The Gods & Goddesses

Norse mythology is painted with a rich palette of gods and goddesses, leaving us a vivid scene of love, betrayal, honor, war and peace. We'll take the briefest glimpse of the most notable deities but firstly we must touch on the families of the gods.

Principally there are the Aesir and the Vanir.

"the differences between them have often been simplified by attributing war and thought to the Aesir, and peace, nature and fertility to the Vanir"
- *Our Troth Volume 1, 2'nd ed.*

Many authors and translators state that there are twelve principal Aesir in addition to **Odin** (goddesses are called Asynjur), which is somewhat murky, as at least two of them are thought to be Vanir and if we include Loki, that brings the tally to thirteen.

1. **Thor** is the foremost of them. He is called Asa-Thor, or Oku-Thor. He is the strongest of all gods and men, and rules over the realm which is called Thrudvang.
2. **Baldr**, who is Odin's second son
3. **Njord**, father to Freyr and Freya and considered to be Vanir
4. **Freyr**, and his sister Freyja were fair of face, and mighty. Freyr is the most famous of the asas. He rules over rain and sunshine, and over the fruits of the earth. It is good to call on him for harvests and peace. He also sways the wealth of men. Freyja is the most famous of the goddesses.
5. **Tyr**. He is very daring and stout-hearted. He sways victory in war, wherefore warriors should call on him.
6. **Bragi** is the name of another of the asas. He is famous for his wisdom, eloquence and flowing speech.
7. **Heimdall** who is also called the white-asa. He is great and holy; born of nine maidens, all of whom were sisters.
8. **Hodir** is the blind asa, but exceedingly strong; the gods would wish that this asa never needed to be named, for the work of his hand will long be kept in memory both by gods and men. (as he unwittingly killed Balder)
9. **Vidar** is the name of the silent asa. He has a very thick shoe, and he is the strongest next after Thor. From him the gods have much help in all hard tasks.

10. **Vali**, is the son of Odin and Rindr. He is daring in combat, and a good shot.

11. **Ullr** is the name of one, who is a son of Sif, and a step-son of Thor. He is so good an archer, and so fast on his skees, that no one can contend with him. He is fair of face, and possesses every quality of a warrior. Men should invoke him in single combat.

12. **Forseti** is a son of Balder and Nanna, Nep's daughter. He has in heaven the hall which hight Glitner. All who come to him with disputes go away perfectly reconciled. Just to listen to People's Future. No better tribunal is to be found among gods and men.

13. **Loki** or Lopt, is numbered among the asas, but whom some call the backbiter of the asas. He is the originator of deceit, and the disgrace of all gods and men. His wife is Sigyn, and their sons are, Nare, or Narfe.

Odin

Odin, Wotan, or Woden was the highest and holiest god of the Northern races. He was the all-pervading spirit of the universe, the personification of the air, the god of universal wisdom and victory, and the leader and protector of princes and heroes. As all the gods were supposed to be descended from him, he was surnamed All-father, and as eldest and chief among them he occupied Asgard, the highest seat; known by the name of **Hlidskialf**, this chair was not only an exalted throne, but also a mighty watch tower, from whence he could overlook the whole world and see at a glance all that was happening among gods, giants, elves, dwarfs, and men.

Figure 75 - "Odhin" (1901) by Johannes Gehrts.

> *" From the hall of Heaven he rode away*
> *To Hlidskialf, and sate upon his throne,*
> *The mount, from whence his eye surveys the world.*
> *And far from Heaven he turn'd his shining orbs*
> *To look on Midgard, and the earth and men."*
> *Balder Dead (Matthew Arnold)*

None but Odin and his wife and queen Frigga had the privilege of using this seat, and when they occupied it they generally gazed towards the south and west, the goal of all Odin's personal the hopes and excursions of the Northern nations.

Odin was generally represented as a tall, vigorous man, about fifty years of age, either with dark curling hair or with a long gray beard and bald head. He was clad in a suit of gray, with a blue hood, and his muscular body was enveloped in a wide blue mantle all flecked with gray—an emblem of the sky with its fleecy clouds. In his hand Odin generally carried the infallible spear **Gungnir**, which was so sacred that an oath sworn upon its point could never be broken, and on his finger or arm he wore the marvelous ring **Draupnir**, the emblem of fruitfulness, precious beyond compare. When seated upon his throne or armed for the fray, in which he often took an active part, Odin wore his eagle helmet; but when he wandered about the earth in human guise, to see what men were doing, he generally donned a broad brimmed hat, drawn down low over his forehead to conceal the fact of his having but one eye.

> *" Then into the Volsungs' dwelling a mighty man there strode,*
> *One-eyed and seeming ancient, yet bright his visage glowed;*
> *Cloud-blue was the hood upon him, and his kirtle gleaming-gray*
> *As the latter morning sun dog'when"the storm is on the way:*
> *A bill he bore on his shoulder, whose mighty ashen beam*
> *Burnt bright with the flame of the sea and the blended silver's gleam."*
> *-   Sigurd The Volsung (William Morris).*

Two ravens, **Hugin** (thought) and **Munin** (memory), perched upon his shoulders as he sat upon his throne, and these he sent out into the wide world every morning, anxiously watching for their return at nightfall, when they whispered into his ears news of all they had seen and heard, keeping him well informed about everything that was happening on earth.

> *" Hugin and Munin*
> *Fly each day*
> *Over the spacious earth.*
> *I fear for Hugin*
> *That he come not back,*
> *Yet more anxious am I for Munin."*

- *Norse Mythology (R. B. Anderson).*

At his feet crouched two wolves or hunting hounds, **Geri** and **Freki**, which animals were therefore considered sacred to him, and of good omen if met by the way. Odin always fed these wolves with his own hands from the meat set before him, for he required no food at all, and seldom tasted anything except the sacred mead.

" Geri and Freki
The war-wont sates,
The triumphant sire of hosts;
But on wine only
The famed in arms
Odin, ever lives."
- Lay Of Grimnir (Thorpe's tr.)

When seated in state upon his throne, Odin rested his feet upon a footstool of gold, the work of the gods, whose furniture and utensils were all fashioned either of that precious metal or of silver.

Besides the magnificent hall **Gladsheim**, where stood the twelve seats occupied by the gods when they met in council, and **Valaskialf**, where his throne, Hlidskialf, was placed, Odin had a third palace in Asgard, situated in the midst of the marvelous grove Glasir, whose leaves were all of shimmering red gold. This palace, called **Valhalla** (the hall of the chosen slain), had five hundred and forty doors, wide enough to allow the passage of eight hundred warriors abreast, and above the principal gate were a boar's head and an eagle whose piercing glance looked all over the world. The walls of this marvelous building were fashioned of glittering spears, so highly polished that they illuminated, all the hall. The roof was of golden shields, and the benches were decorated with fine armor, the god's gifts to his guests. Here long tables afforded ample accommodations for the warriors fallen in battle, who were called **Einheriar**, and were considered Odin's favorite guests.

" Easily to be known is,
By those who to Odin come,
The mansion by its aspect.
Its roof with spears is laid,
Its hall with shields is decked,
With corselets are its benches strewed."
- Lay Of Grimnir (Thorpe's tr.)

Figure 76 - "Walhalla" (1905) by Emil Doepler.

Thor

According to some mythologists, Thor, or **Donar**, (also Asa-Thor) is the son of Jord (Erda , Iorth, or mother earth), and of Odin, but others state that his mother was Frigga, queen of the gods. This child was very remarkable for his great size and strength, and very soon after his birth amazed the assembled gods by playfully lifting and throwing about ten loads of bear skins. Although generally good tempered, Thor occasionally flew into a terrible rage, and as he was very dangerous under these circumstances, his mother, unable to control him, sent him away from home and entrusted him to the care of Vingnir (the winged), and of Hlora (heat). These foster parents, who are also considered as the personification of Thor's sheet lightning, soon managed to control their trouble-some charge, and brought him up so wisely, that all the gods were duly grateful for their kind offices. Thor himself, recognizing all he owed them, assumed the names of Vingthor and Hlorridi (the Fire-driver or ride), by which he is also known. Having attained his full growth and the age of reason, Thor was admitted in Asgard among the other gods, where he occupied one of the twelve seats in the great judgment hall. He was also given the realm of **Thrud-vang** or Thrud-heim, where he built a wonderful palace called **Bilskirnir** (lightning), the most spacious in all Asgard. It contained five hundred and forty halls for the accommodation of the thralls, who after death were welcomed to his home, where they were treated as well as their masters in Valhalla, for Thor was the patron god of the peasants and lower classes.

> *" Five hundred halls*
> *And forty more,*
> *Methinketh, hath*
> *Bowed Bilskirnir.*
> *Of houses roofed*
> *There's none I know*
> *My son's surpassing."*
> *- Saemund's Edda (Percy's tr.).*

As he was god of thunder, Thor alone was never allowed to pass over the wonderful bridge Bifrost, lest he should set it aflame by the heat of his presence; and when he daily wished to join his fellow gods by the Urdar fountain, under the shade of the sacred tree Yggdrasil, he was forced to make his way thither on foot, wading through the rivers Kormt and Ormt, and the two streams Kerlaug, to the trysting place.

Figure 77 - Thor wades through rivers while the rest of the æsir ride across Bifröst (1895) by Lorenz Frølich.

Thor, who was honored as the highest god in Norway, came second in the trilogy of all the other countries, and was called " old Thor," because he is supposed by some mythologists to have belonged to an older dynasty of gods, and not on account of his actual age, for he was represented and described as a man in his prime, tall and well formed, with muscular limbs and bristling red hair and beard, from which, in moments of anger, the sparks fairly flew.

> *" First, Thor with the bent brow,*
> *In red beard muttering low,*
>
> *Darting fierce lightnings from eyeballs that glow,*
> *Comes, while each chariot wheel*
> *Echoes in thunder peal,*
>
> *As his dread hammer shock*
> *Makes Earth and Heaven rock,*
> *Clouds rifting above, while Earth quakes below."*
>
> \- *Valhalla (J. C. Jones).*

The Northern races further adorned him with a crown, on each point of which was either a glittering star, or a steadily burning flame, so that his head was ever surrounded by a kind of halo of fire, his own element.

Thor was the proud possessor of a magic hammer called Miolnir (the crusher) which he hurled at his enemies, the frost giants, with destructive power, and which hammer, possessed the wonderful property of always returning to his hand, however far away he might hurl it.

> *" I am the Thunderer!*
> *Here in my Northland,*
> *My fastness and fortress,*
> *Reign I forever!*
>
> *" Here amid icebergs*
> *Rule I the nations;*
> *This is my hammer,*
> *Miolnir the mighty;*
> *Giants and sorcerers*
> *Cannot withstand it! "*
> *- Saga Of King Olaf (Longfellow).*

As this huge hammer, the emblem of the thunderbolts, was generally red hot, the god had an iron gauntlet called **Iarn-greiper**, which enabled him to grasp it firmly and hurl it very far, his strength, which was already remarkable, being always doubled when he wore his magic belt called **Megin-giord**.

" This is my girdle:
Whenever I brace it,
Strength is redoubled ! "

- Saga Of King Olaf (Longfellow).

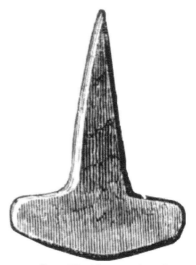

Figure 78 - A hammer shaped amulet of silver, found in Fitjar, Hordaland, Norway

Thor's hammer **Mjolnir** was considered so very sacred by the ancient Northern people, that they were wont to make the sign of the hammer, as the Christians later taught them to make the sign of the cross, to ward off all evil influences, and to secure many, blessings. The same sign was also made over the newly born infant when water was poured over its head and a name given it. The hammer was used to drive in boundary stakes, which it was considered sacrilegious to remove, to hallow the threshold of a new house, to solemnize a marriage, and, lastly, to consecrate the funeral pyre upon which the bodies of heroes were burned, together with their weapons and steeds, and, in some cases, with their wives and dependents.

In Sweden, Thor, like Odin, was supposed to wear a broad brimmed hat, and hence the storm clouds in that country are known as Thor's hat, a name also given to one of the principal mountains in Norway. The rumble and roar of the thunder were called the roll of his chariot, for he alone among the gods never rode on horseback, but walked, or drove in a brazen chariot drawn by two goats,

Tanngniostr (tooth cracker), and **Tanngrisnr** (tooth gnasher), from whose teeth and hoofs the sparks constantly flew.

> *" Thou earnest near the next, O warrior Thor!*
> *Shouldering thy hammer, in thy chariot drawn,*
> *Swaying the long-hair'd goats with silver'd rein."*

- *Balder Dead (Matthew Arnold).*

When the god thus drove about from place to place, he was called Aku-thor, or Thor the charioteer, and in southern Germany the people, fancying a brazen chariot alone inadequate to furnish all the noise they heard, declared it was loaded with copper kettles, which rattled and clashed, and therefore often called him, with disrespectful familiarity, the kettle vender.

Figure 79 - "Thor" (1901) by Johannes Gehrts.

Thor was twice married; first to the giantess **Iarnsaxa** (iron stone), who bore him two sons, **Magni** (strength) and **Modi** Thor's (courage), both destined to survive their father and family. the twilight of the gods, and rule over the new world which was to rise like a phoenix from the ashes of the first.

His second wife was **Sif**, the golden-haired, who also bore him two children, **Lorride**, and a daughter named **Thrud**, a young giantess renowned for her size and strength.

Baldr

Baldr is Odin's second son (by Frigg); he is the best and is praised by all. He is so fair of aspect, and so bright, that light issues from him. He is the wisest, and most eloquent, and most amiable of the Aesir.

According to Gylfaginning, a book of **Snorri Sturluson's** Prose Edda, Baldr's wife is **Nanna** and their son is Forseti. In Gylfaginning, Snorri relates that Baldr had the greatest ship ever built,

Figure 80 - "Balder the Good" (1900) by Jacques Reich.

named **Hringhorni**, and that there is no place more beautiful than his hall, **Breidablik**.

Baldr is known primarily for the story of his death which is seen as the first in the chain of events which will ultimately lead to the destruction of the gods at Ragnarok. Baldr will be reborn in the new world, according to Voluspa.

Figure 81 - Death of Baldr as depicted on a Faroe Islands postage stamp (2003) by Anker Eli Petersen.

Njord

Father to Freya and Frey (by his unamed Van sister), Njord is of the Vanir, and dwells in Noatun. He rules the course of the wind, stills the ocean, and quenches fire. He is invoked by sea-farers and fishermen, and is the patron of temples and altars. He is so rich that he can give wealth and superfluity to those that invoke him.

Married to Skadi, he longs for the sea when with her in her mountain abode.

Figure 82 - "Njörd's desire of the Sea" (1908) by W. G. Collingwood.

Freyr

Freyr (Frey), a son of Niord, was also bred in Vanaheim. He is beloved of all, and is one of the most renowned of the Aesir. He presides over rain, and sunshine, and the fruits of the earth. He is to be invoked for good seasons and peace. He also presides over the wealth of men. He is the god of the year, and giver of cattle, and loosens the bonds of the captive. In the beginning of time, Alf heim was given to him by the gods as tooth-money. He reigns over the Light-elves (Ljosalfar), who are more beauteous than the sun, while the Black or Dark-elves (Svartalfar), who are blacker than pitch, dwell in the bowels of the earth. He is the foe and sayer of Beli; is the owner of **Skidbladnir**, and rides a chariot drwan by the Boar **Gulinbursti** (golden bristles).

Figure 83 - "Freyr" (1901) by Johannes Gehrts.

Tyr

Tyr, is the boldest and stoutest of the Aesir. It is he who gives victory in war, and should be invoked by warriors. It is a proverbial saying, that a man who surpasses others in valor is *as bold as Tyr*. He is also so wise, that it is usual to say of a very sagacious man, he is *as wise as Tyr*. He is, however, not considered as a settler of quarrels among people. Odin is his father, but on his mother's side he is of giant race.

Figure 84 - Tyr feeds Fenrir (1909) by Charles Huard

Bragi

Bragi is another of the Aesir. He is famed for wisdom and eloquence, and is profoundly skilled in the art of poetry, which from him is denominated bragr, and those who distinguish themselves above others in eloquence are called bragr-men, and bragr-women. He is upbraided by Loki for not being sufficiently

Figure 85 - Bragi

warlike and doughty in battle. He has a long beard, and is a son of Odin.

210

Heimdall

Heimdall, though regarded as a Van, is nevertheless called a son of Odin. He is also called the White or Bright God, and is a great and holy god. In the beginning of time he was born, on the boundary of the earth, of nine giant maidens, who were sisters, and was nourished with the strength of the earth, and the cold sea. The nine maidens were named, Gialp, Greip, Elgia, Angeia, Ulfrun, Aurgiafa, Sindur, Atla, and Jarnsaxa. He drinks mead in his bright hall, Himinbjorg, by Bifrost, at the bridge head, where the rainbow reaches heaven. There he sits, as the watchman of the gods, at the end of heaven, to guard the bridge from the mountain giants, where he is often wetted through with rain, or, as Loki expresses it, gets a wet back. He needs less sleep than a bird, hears the grass grow on the ground and the wool on the sheep, and sees, as well by night as by

day, for a hundred miles around him. His horn Gioll (Gjallarhorn) is hidden under the sacred tree Yggdrasil; but when he blows it, its sound is heard through all worlds. Heimdall's horse is named **Gulltopp** (Gold-mane). He is himself also called Hallinskeidi (Descending), and Gullintanni (Golden-tooth), because his teeth are of gold. The head is called Heimdall's sword, because he was pierced through with a man's head. He contended with Loki for the **Brisinga-men,** Freyia's

Figure 86 - Heimdall (1895) depicted with Gjallarhorn by Lorenz Frølich.

1

ornament.

Hoder

Hoder (hod) is another of the Aesir, and is said to be a son of Odin. He is blind, but exceedingly strong. The gods may well wish never to hear his name pronounced, for his deed will be long remembered both by gods and men.

Vidar

Vidar is called the silent god. He is the son of Odin and the giantess Grid (Grror). He has a very thick shoe, that has been forming, from the beginning of time, of the thin shreds that are cut from shoes in shaping the toes or heels: therefore should every one cast away such shreds, who cares about rendering aid to the Aesir. In other places mention is made of his iron shoes, and in the Skalda he is called eiganda iarnskoss (owner of the iron shoe). He is the strongest of the gods after Thor, and affords them aid in many difficulties. His abode, **Landvidi**, is thickly overgrown with brushwood and high grass.

Figure 87 - A depiction of Víðarr stabbing Fenrir while holding his jaws apart (1908) by W. G. Collingwood

Vali

Vali is a son of Odin and **Rind**. He is stout in battle, and an excellent archer. He was birthed for the sole purpose of killing Hoder as revenge for Hoder's accidental murder of his half-brother, Baldr. He grew to full adulthood within one day of his birth, and slew Hoder. Vali is fated to survive Ragnarok.

The Vali myth is referred to in Baldrs draumar:

Rindr will bear Váli
in western halls;
that son of Óðinn
will kill when one night old—
he will not wash hand,
nor comb head,
before he bears to the pyre
Baldr's adversary.

213

- Ursula Dronke's translation

And in Voluspa:

There formed from that stem,
which was slender-seeming,
a shaft of anguish, perilous:
Hǫðr started shooting.
A brother of Baldr
was born quickly:
he started—Óðinn's son—
slaying, at one night old.

There is another Vali, a son of Loki by Sigyn, who was transformed by the gods into a slavering wolf who tore out the throat of his brother Narfi to punish Loki for his crimes.

Ullr

(Ull) is the son of Sif and stepson of Thor. He is a good archer, and runs so rapidly on snow-shoes, that no one is a match for him. He is handsome, and warlike in habit and manners. It is good to invoke him in single combats. His dwelling is Ydal (Ydalir).

Forseti

A son of Balder and Nanna, Nef's (Nep's) daughter, dwells in the heavenly mansion called **Glitnir**, which is supported on gold, and roofed with silver. He settles all quarrels, and neither gods nor men know any better judgments than his.

Loki

Loki is Aesir or jötunn (or both). His father is the giant Farbauti; his mother is Laufey (leafy-isle), or Nal (needle), and his brothers are Byleist and Helblindi. He is father to Hel, the **Fenrir** wolf and the **Jormungandr** world serpent.

Loki's relation with the gods varies by source. Loki assists the gods, and sometimes causes problems for them. Loki is a shape shifter and in separate incidents he appears in the form of a salmon and a mare. Loki's positive relations with the gods ends with his role in engineering the death of the god Baldr. Loki is eventually bound by the gods with the entrails of one of his sons. A serpent drips venom from above him that his wife Sigyn collects into a bowl. However, Sigyn must empty the bowl when it

Figure 89- "Loki Bound (motive from the Gosforth Cross)" (1908) by W. G. Collingwood.

215

is full, and the venom that drips in the mean time causes Loki to writhe in pain, thereby causing earthquakes. During the events of Ragnarok, Loki is foretold to fight against the gods among the forces of the jötnar. There, he will encounter the god Heimdall and the two will slay each other.

Frigg

Frigg (sometimes anglicized as Frigga) is said to be the wife of Odin, and is the "foremost among the goddesses" and the queen of Asgard. Frigg appears primarily in Norse mythological stories as a wife and a mother. She is also described as having the power of prophecy yet she does not reveal what she knows. Frigg is described as the only one other than Odin who is permitted to sit on his high seat Hlidskjalf and look out over the universe. Her habitation is **Fensalir**.

Figure 90 - A depiction of Fulla kneeling beside her mistress, Frigg, (1865) by Ludwig Pietsch.

She possesses a feathergarb, or falcon's plumage.

Frigg's children are Baldr and Hoder, her stepchildren are Thor, Hermodr, Heimdall, Tyr, Vidar, Vali, and Skjoldr. Frigg's companion is **Eir**, a goddess associated with medical skills. Frigg's attendants are **Hlin**, **Gna**, and **Fulla**.

The English term Friday derives from the Anglo-Saxon name for Frigg, Frige.

Freya

In equal veneration to Frigg, is Freya, the daughter of Njord and sister of Frey. From her descent, she is called Vana-dis, or goddess of the Vanir. She dwells in **Folkvang**, her hall is called Sessrumnir (roomy-seated); and when she rides to battle, one half of the slain belong to her, the other to Odin; hence her appellation of Valfreyia. She delights in love songs, and is to be prayed to in love matters. When she rides, her chariot is drawn by two cats. She owns the ornament called Brising, or Brisinga-men. Like Frigg, she possesses a falcon's plumage, and, like Frey, a hog named Gullinbursti, or Hildisvini (the swine of war), which the dwarfs Dain and Nabbi made for her, and whose golden bristles illuminate the

Figure 91- "Freya" (1901) by Johannes Gehrts. The goddess Freya rests her hand upon a shield.

thickest darkness. Freya was married to Od, and they had a daughter named Hnos, after whose name all precious things are called hnosir. Od forsook her, and went far away: she weeps for his absence, and her tears are red gold. She travelled among unknown people in search of him. Freya has many names, because she assumed a new one among each people that she visited in her journeys: hence she is called Mardoll, Horn, Gefn, and Syr.

Idunna

Idunna (Idun), the wife of Bragi, and daughter of Ivald, keeps in her casket the apples which the gods must eat when they begin to grow old: they then again become young; and this process will continue till the destruction of the gods, or Ragnarok. Her dwelling is in Brunnakr.

Figure 92 - "Loki and Idun" (1911) by John Bauer

Sif

Figure 94 - Sif (1909) by John Charles Dollman

Sif, Thor's wife, mother of Ullr and Thrud, has a noble head of hair. Sif is associated with the earth with famously golden hair which is said to have been shorn by Loki. Thor forces Loki to have a golden headpiece made for Sif, resulting in not only Sif's golden tresses but also five other objects for other gods.

Scholars have proposed that Sif's hair may represent fields of golden wheat and that she may be associated with fertility, family, wedlock and/or that she is connected to rowan.

Saga

Saga dwells in Sokkvabekkr[31], over which the cool waves murmur. There she and Odin joyful drink each day from golden cups.

Figure 95 - Sága and Odin converse while holding cups in an illustration (1895) by Lorenz Frølich.

---

[31] Old Norse; "sunken bank", "sunken bench", or "treasure bank

Gefjon

Gefjon is a goddess associated with ploughing, the Danish island of Zealand, the legendary early Swedish king Gylfi, the king Skjöldr, and virginity. She knows the decrees of fate as well as Odin himself, and all who die a virgin become her attendants. Heimskringla notes that Gefjon married king Skjöldr.

Figure 96 - Gefjun Plows Zealand with her Oxen (1882) by Karl Ehrenberg

Other Goddesses

🔺 **Gna** rides through the air and over the sea, on Frigg's messages, on the horse **Hofvarpnir**[32]. Once, as she was riding, some Vanir saw her in the air, one of whom said,

> *What flies there ?*
> *what goes there ?*
> *or is borne in air ?*
> *She answered,*
> *I fly not,*
> *though I go,*
> *and am borne in air,*
> *on Hofvarpnir,*
> *that Hamskerpir*
> *got by Gardarofa.*

🔺 **Sjofn** inclines the mind of both sexes to love: from her name a lover is called siafni.

🔺 **Lofn**[33] is kind and good to those that invoke her: she has permission from All-father or Frigg to unite those who love each other, whatever hindrances or difficulties may stand in the way. From her name is derived the word lof (praise, leave), because she is greatly praised by men.

🔺 **Vor** hears the oaths and vows of lovers, and punishes those who break them. She is wise, and hears of everything, so that nothing can be hidden from her.

🔺 **Syn**[34] guards the door of the hall, and locks it against those that may not enter. She is appointed as the defender in courts of those causes which it is endeavored to defeat by falsehood.

🔺 **Snotra**[35] is sagacious (wise) and of elegant manners. From her name a man or woman of sagacity is said to be snotr.

---

[32] ON "he who throws his hoofs about", "hoof-thrower" or "hoof kicker"
[33] ON "comforter," or "loving"
[34] ON "refusal"
[35] ON "clever"

🔺 **Sol**[36] or **Sunna**[37], is the sister of Sinthgunt, sister of Mani, the daughter of Mundilfari, and wife to Glenr. She is foretold to be killed by a monstrous wolf during the events of Ragnarök, though beforehand she will have given birth to a daughter who continues her mother's course through the heavens.

🔺 **Jorth**[38] (Earth) is a female jotunn, the mother of Thor and Meili, and the personification of the Earth. Fjörgyn and Hlôdyn are considered to be other names for Jörð.

🔺 **Rind**, the mother of Vali.

🔺 **Eir** is the best leech (medical skill).

🔺 **Hlin** guards those whom Frigg is desirous of freeing from peril. She is called upon when in despair.

🔺 **Fulla** is a maiden with disheveled hair and a golden band round her head. She bears Frigg's casket, has charge of her foot-covering, and knows her secret council.

🔺 **Hel or** Hella, daughter of Loki, and appointed by Odin to rule Hellheim is given a portion of the dead. She is half-black and half-flesh colored, and has a gloomy, down-cast appearance.

---

[36] ON "sun"
[37] OHG "sun"
[38] ON "earth"

Chapter 8 – Tao of the North

ome consider the Havamal the **"Tao of the North"** – the Northern way if you will. **The Havamal** ("Sayings of the high one") is presented as a single poem in the Poetic Edda. The poem, itself a combination of different poems, largely presents advice for living and survival composed around the central figure of Odin. Havamal is both practical and metaphysical in content; this is particularly apparent towards the end of the poem, as the poem shifts into an account of Odin's obtaining of the runic alphabet and obscure text relating to various charms and spells Odin knows.

The only surviving source for the Havamal is contained within the 13th century Codex Regius, and is thought to be no older than from around the year 800 AD (though derived from an earlier oral tradition).

Figure 97 - Chinese Symbol for Tao, or "The Way"

Old Northern Ethics for Life[39]

"....most of the "Havamal" is a collection of ethical teaching. All that has been preserved by it has been published and translated by

---

[39] From as essay to his students in Japan - Patrick Lafcadio Hearn (27 June 1850 – 26 September 1904), also known as Koizumi Yakumo (小泉八雲) after gaining Japanese citizenship, was an author, best known for his books about Japan. He is especially well-known for his collections of Japanese legends and ghost stories, such as Kwaidan: Stories and Studies of Strange Things.

Professors Vigfusson and Powell. It is very old—perhaps the oldest Northern literature that we have. I am going to attempt a short lecture upon it, because it is very closely related to the subject of Northern character, and will help us, perhaps better than almost anything else, to understand how the ancestors of the English felt and thought before they became Christians. Nor is this all. I venture to say that the character of the modern English people still retains much more of the quality indicated by the "Havamal" than of the quality implied by Christianity. **The old Northern gods are not dead; they rule a very great part of the world to-day.**

The proverbial philosophy of a people helps us to understand more about them than any other kind of literature. And this sort of literature is certainly among the oldest. It represents only the result of human experience in society, the wisdom that men get by contact with each other, the results of familiarity with right and wrong. By studying the proverbs of a people, you can always make a very good guess as to whether you could live comfortably among them or not.

Froude, in one of his sketches of travel in Norway, made the excellent observation that if -we could suddenly go back to the time of the terrible sea-kings, if we could revisit to-day the homes of the old Northern pirates, and find them exactly as they were one thousand or fifteen hundred years ago, we should find them very much like the modern Englishmen—big, simple, silent men, concealing a great deal of shrewdness under an aspect of simplicity. The teachings of the "Havamal" give great force to this supposition. The book must have been known in some form to the early English—or at least the verses composing it (it is all written in verse) ; and as I have already said, the morals of the old English, as well as their character, differed very little from those of the men of the still further North, with whom they mingled and intermarried freely, both before and after the Danish conquest, when for one moment England and Sweden were one kingdom.

Of course you must remember that Northern society was a very terrible thing in some ways. Every man carried his life in his hands; every farmer kept sword and spear at his side even in his own fields; and every man expected to die fighting. In fact, among the men of the more savage North—the men of Norway in especial—it was considered a great disgrace to die of sickness, to die on one's bed. That was not to die like a man. Men would go out and get themselves killed, when they felt old age or sickness coming on. But these facts must not blind us to the other fact that there was even in that society a great force of moral cohesion, and sound principles of morality. If there had not been, it could not have existed; much less could the people who lived under it have become the masters of a great part of the world, which they are at the present day. There was, in spite of all that fierceness, much kindness and good nature among them; there were rules of conduct such as no man could find fault with—rules which still govern English society to some extent. And there was opportunity enough for social amusement, social enjoyment, and the winning of public esteem by a noble life.

Still, even in the "Havamal," one is occasionally startled by teachings which show the darker side of Northern life, a life of perpetual vendetta. As in old Japan, no man could live under the same heaven with the murderer of his brother or father; vengeance was a duty even in the case of a friend. On the subject of enemies the "Havamal" gives not a little curious advice :

A man should never step a foot beyond his weapons; for he can never tell where, on his path without, he may need his spear.
A man, before he goes into a house, should look to and espy all the doorways (so that he can find his way out quickly again), for he can never know where foes may be sitting in another man's house.

Does not this remind us of the Japanese proverb that everybody has three enemies outside of his own door? But the meaning of the "Havamal" teaching is much more sinister. And when the man goes into the house, he is still told to be extremely watchful—to keep his ears and eyes open so that he may not be taken by surprise:

225

The wary guest keeps watchful silence; he listens with his ears and peers about with his eyes; thus does every wise man look about him.

One would think that men must have had very strong nerves to take comfort under such circumstances, but the poet tells us that the man who can enjoy nothing must be both a coward and a fool. Although a man was to keep watch to protect his life, that was not a reason why he should be afraid of losing it. There were but three things of which a man should be particularly afraid. The first was drink—because drink often caused a man to lose control of his temper; the second was another man's wife—repeatedly the reader is warned never to make love to another man's wife; and the third was thieves—men who would pretend friendship for the purpose of killing and stealing. The man who could keep constant watch over himself and his surroundings was, of course, likely to have the longest life.

Now in all countries there is a great deal of ethical teaching, and always has been, on the subject of speech. The "Havamal" is full of teaching on this subject—the necessity of silence, the danger and the folly of reckless talk. You all know the Japanese proverb that "the mouth is the front gate of all misfortune." The Norse poet puts the same truth into a grimmer shape: "The tongue works death to the head." Here are a number of sayings on this subject:

He that is never silent talks much folly; a glib tongue, unless it be bridled, will often talk a man into trouble.

Do not speak three angry words with a worse man; for often the better man falls by the worse man's sword.

Smile thou in the face of the man thou trustest not, and speak against thy mind.

This is of course a teaching of cunning; but it is the teaching, however immoral, that rules in English society to-day. In the old Norse, however, there were many reasons for having a quarrel whenever possible—reasons which must have existed also in feudal

226

Japan. A man might not care about losing his own life; but he had to be careful not to stir up a feud that might go on for a hundred years. Although there was a great deal of killing, killing always remained a serious matter, because for every killing there had to be a vengeance. It is true that the law exonerated the man who killed another, if he paid a certain blood-price; murder was not legally considered an unpardonable crime. But the family of the dead man would very seldom be satisfied with a payment; they would want blood for blood. Accordingly men had to be very cautious about quarreling, however brave they might personally be.

But all this caution about silence and about watchfulness did not mean that a man should be unable to speak to the purpose when speech was required. "A wise man," says the "Havamal," "should be able both to ask and to answer." There is a proverb which you know, to the effect that you cannot shut the door upon another man's mouth. So says the Norse poet:

"The sons of men can keep silence about nothing that passes among men; therefore a man should be able to take his own part, prudently and strongly."

Says the "Havamal":

"A fool thinks he knows everything if he sits snug in his little corner; but he is at a loss for words if the people put to him a question."

Elsewhere it is said:
"Arch dunce is he who can speak nought, for that is the mark of a fool." And the sum of all this teaching about the tongue is that men should never speak without good reason, and then should speak to the point strongly and wisely.

On the subject of fools there is a great deal in the "Havamal"; but you must understand always by the word fool, in the Northern sense, a man of weak character who knows not what to do in time of difficulty. That was a fool among those men, and a dangerous fool;

for in such a state of society mistakes in act or in speech might reach to terrible consequences. See these little observations about fools:

Open-handed, bold-hearted men live most happily, they never feel care; but a fool troubles himself about everything. The niggard pines for gifts.

A fool is awake all night, worrying about everything; when the morning comes he is worn out, and all his troubles are just the same as before.

A fool thinks that all who smile upon him are his friends, not knowing, when he is with wise men, who there may be plotting against him.

If a fool gets a drink, all his mind is immediately displayed.

But it was not considered right for a man not to drink, although drink was a dangerous thing. On the contrary, not to drink would have been thought a mark of cowardice and of incapacity for self-control. A man was expected even to get drunk if necessary, and to keep his tongue and his temper no matter how much he drank. The strong character would only become more cautious and more silent under the influence of drink; the weak man would immediately show his weakness. I am told the curious fact that in the English army at the present day officers are expected to act very much after the teaching of the old Norse poet; a man is expected to be able on occasion to drink a considerable amount of wine or spirits without showing the effects of it, either in his conduct or in his speech. "Drink thy share of mead; speak fair or not at all"—that was the old text, and a very sensible one in its way.

Laughter was also condemned, if indulged in without very good cause. "The miserable man whose mind is warped laughs at everything, not knowing what he ought to know, that he himself has no lack of faults." I need scarcely tell you that the English are still a very serious people, not disposed to laugh nearly so much as are the men of the more sympathetic Latin races. You will remember perhaps Lord Chesterfield's saying that since he became a man no man had ever seen him laugh. I remember about twenty years ago that there was published by some Englishman a very learned and very interesting little book, called "The Philosophy of Laughter," in which it was gravely asserted that all laughter was foolish. I must acknowledge, however, that no book ever made me laugh more than the volume in question. The great virtue of the men of the North, according to the "Havamal," was indeed the virtue which has given to the English race its present great position among nations,—the simplest of all virtues, common sense. But common sense means much more than the words might imply to the Japanese students, or to any one unfamiliar with English idioms. Common sense, or mother-wit, means natural intelligence, as opposed to, and independent of, cultivated or educated intelligence. It means inherited knowledge; and inherited knowledge may take even the form of genius. It means foresight. It means intuitive knowledge of other people's character. It means cunning as well as broad comprehension. And the modern Englishman, in all times and in all countries, trusts especially to this faculty, which is very largely developed in the race to which he belongs. No Englishman believes in working from book learning. He suspects all theories, philosophical or other. He suspects everything new, and dislikes it, unless he can be compelled by the force of circumstances to see that this new thing has advantages over the old. Race-experience is what he invariably depends upon, whenever he can, whether in India, in Egypt, or in Australia. His statesmen do not consult historical precedents in order to decide what to do: they first learn the facts as they are; then they depend upon their own common sense, not at all upon their university learning or upon philosophical theories. And in the case of the English nation, it must be acknowledged that this instinctive method has been eminently successful. When the "Havamal" speaks of wisdom it means mother-wit, and nothing else; indeed, there was no reading or writing to speak of in those times:

No man can carry better baggage on his journey than wisdom.

There is no better friend than great common sense.

But the wise man should not show himself to be wise without occasion. He should remember that the majority of men are not wise, and he should be careful not to show his superiority over them unnecessarily. Neither should he despise men who do not happen to be as wise as himself:

No man is so good but there is a flaw in him, nor so bad as to be good for nothing.

Middling wise should every man be; never overwise. Those who know many things rarely lead the happiest life.

Middling wise should every man be; never overwise. No man should know his fate beforehand; so shall he live freest from care.

Middling wise should every man be, never too wise. A wise man's heart is seldom glad, if its owner be a true sage.

This is the ancient wisdom also of Solomon: "He that increases wisdom increases sorrow." But how very true as worldly wisdom these little Northern sentences are. That a man who knows a little of many things, and no one thing perfectly, is the happiest man—this certainly is even more true to-day than it was a thousand years ago. Spencer has well observed that the man who can influence his generation, is never the man greatly in advance of his time, but only the man who is very slightly better than his fellows. The man who is very superior is likely to be ignored or disliked. Mediocrity can not help disliking superiority; and as the old Northern sage declared, "the average of men is but moiety." Moiety does not mean necessarily mediocrity, but also that which is below mediocrity. What we call in England to-day, as Matthew Arnold called it, the Philistine element, continues to prove in our own time, to almost every superior man, the danger of being too wise.

Interesting in another way, and altogether more agreeable, are the old sayings about friendship: "Know this, if thou hast a trusty friend, go and see him often; because a road which is seldom trod gets choked with brambles and high grass."

Be not thou the first to break off from thy friend. Sorrow will eat thy heart if thou lackest the friend to open thy heart to.

Anything is better than to be false; he is no friend who only speaks to please.

Which means, of course, that a true friend is not afraid to find fault with his friend's course; indeed, that is his solemn duty. But these teachings about friendship are accompanied with many cautions; for one must be very careful in the making of friends. The ancient Greeks had a terrible proverb:

"Treat your friend as if he should become some day your enemy; and treat your enemy as if he might some day become your friend."

This proverb seems to me to indicate a certain amount of doubt in human nature. We do not find this doubt in the Norse teaching, but on the contrary, some very excellent advice. The first thing to remember is that friendship is sacred: "He that opens his heart to another mixes blood with him." Therefore one should be very careful either about forming or about breaking a friendship.

A man should be a friend to his friend's friend. But no man should be a friend of his friend's foe, nor of his foe's friend.

A man should be a friend with his friend, and pay back gift with gift; give back laughter for laughter (to his enemies), and lesing for lies.

Give and give back makes the longest friend. Give not overmuch at one time. Gift always looks for return.

The poet also tells us how trifling gifts are quite sufficient to make friends and to keep them, if wisely given. A costly gift may seem like a bribe; a little gift is only the sign of kindly feeling. And as a mere matter of justice, a costly gift may be unkind, for it puts the friend under an obligation which he may not be rich enough to repay. Repeatedly we are told also that too much should not be expected of friendship. The value of a friend is his affection, his sympathy; but favours that cost must always be returned.

I never met a man so open-hearted and free with his food, but that boon was boon to him—nor so generous as not to look for return if he had a chance.

Emerson says almost precisely the same thing in his essay on friendship—showing how little human wisdom has changed in all the centuries. Here is another good bit of advice concerning visits:

It is far away to an ill friend, even though he live on one's road; but to a good friend there is a short cut, even though he live far out.

Go on, be not a guest ever in the same house. The welcome becomes wearisome if he sits too long at another's table.

This means that we must not impose on our friends; but there is a further caution on the subject of eating at a friend's house. You must not go to your friend's house hungry, when you can help it.

A man should take his meal betimes, before he goes to his neighbour—or he will sit and seem hungered like one starving, and have no power to talk.

That is the main point to remember in dining at another's house, that you are not there only for your own pleasure, but for that of other people. You are expected to talk; and you cannot talk if you are very hungry. At this very day a gentleman makes it the rule to do the same thing. Accordingly we see that these rough men of the North must have had a good deal of social refinement—refinement not of dress or of speech, but of feeling. Still, says the poet, one's own home is the best, though it be but a cottage. "A man is a man in his own house."

Now we come to some sentences teaching caution, which are noteworthy in a certain way:

Tell one man thy secret, but not two. What three men know, all the world knows.

Never let a bad man know thy mishaps; for from a bad man thou shalt never get reward for thy sincerity.

I shall presently give you some modern examples in regard to the advice concerning bad men. Another thing to be cautious about is praise. If you have to be careful about blame, you must be very cautious also about praise.

Praise the day at even-tide; a woman at her burying; a sword when it has been tried; a maid when she is married; ice when you have crossed over it; ale when it is drunk.

If there is anything noteworthy in English character to-day it is the exemplification of this very kind of teaching. This is essentially Northern. The last people from whom praise can be expected, even for what is worthy of all praise, are the English. A new friendship, a new ideal, a reform, a noble action, a wonderful poet, an exquisite painting—any of these things will be admired and praised by every other people in Europe long before you can get Englishmen to praise. The Englishman all this time is studying, considering, trying to find fault. Why should he try to find fault? So that he will not make any mistakes at a later day. He has inherited the terrible caution of his ancestors in regard to mistakes. It must be granted that his caution has saved him from a number of very serious mistakes that other nations have made. It must also be acknowledged that he exercises a fair amount of moderation in the opposite direction—this modern Englishman; he has learned caution of another kind, which his ancestors taught him. "Power," says the "Havamal," "should be used with moderation; for whoever finds himself among valiant men will discover that no man is peerless." And this is a very important thing for the strong man to know—that however strong, he can not be the strongest; his match will be found when occasion demands it. Not only Scandinavian but English rulers have often discovered this fact to their cost. Another matter to be very anxious about is public opinion.

Chattels die; kinsmen pass away; one dies oneself; but I know something that never dies—the name of the man, for good or bad.

Do not think that this means anything religious. It means only that the reputation of a man goes to influence the good or ill fortune of his descendants. It is something to be proud of, to be the son of a good man; it helps to success in life. On the other hand, to have had a father of ill reputation is a very serious obstacle to success of any kind in countries where the influence of heredity is strongly recognized.

I have nearly exhausted the examples of this Northern wisdom which I selected for you; but there are two subjects which remain to be considered. One is the law of conduct in regard to misfortune; and the other is the rule of conduct in regard to women. A man was expected to keep up a brave heart under any circumstances. These old Northmen seldom committed suicide; and I must tell you that all the talk about Christianity having checked the practice of suicide to some extent, cannot be fairly accepted as truth. In modern England to-day the suicides average nearly three thousand a year; but making allowances for extraordinary circumstances, it is certain that the Northern races consider suicide in an entirely different way from what the Latin races do. There was very little suicide among the men of the North, because every man considered it his duty to get killed, not to kill himself; and to kill himself would have seemed cowardly, as implying fear of being killed by others. In modern ethical training, quite apart from religious considerations, a man is taught that suicide is only excusable in case of shame, or under such exceptional circumstances as have occurred in the history of the Indian mutiny. At all events, we have the feeling still strongly manifested in England that suicide is not quite manly; and this is certainly due much more to ancestral habits of thinking, which date back to pagan days, than to Christian doctrine. As I have said, the pagan English would not commit suicide to escape mere pain. But the Northern people knew how to die to escape shame. There is an awful story in Roman history about the wives and daughters of the conquered German tribes, thousands in number, asking to be promised that their virtue should be respected, and all killing themselves when the Roman general refused the request. No Southern people of Europe in that time would have shown such heroism upon such a matter. Leaving honour aside, however, the old book tells us that a man should never despair.

Fire, the sight of the sun, good health, and a blameless life,—these are the goodliest things in this world.

Yet a man is not utterly wretched, though he have bad health, or be maimed.

The halt may ride a horse; the handless may drive a herd; the deaf can fight and do well; better be blind than buried. A corpse is good for naught.

On the subject of women there is not very much in the book beyond the usual caution in regard to wicked women; but there is this little observation:

Never blame a woman for what is all man's weakness. Hues charming and fair may move the wise and not the dullard. Mighty love turns the son of men from wise to fool.

This is shrewd, and it contains a very remarkable bit of esthetic truth, that it requires a wise man to see certain kinds of beauty, which a stupid man could never be made to understand. And, leaving aside the subject of love, what very good advice it is never to laugh at a person for what can be considered a common failure. In the same way an intelligent man should learn to be patient with the unintelligent, as the same poem elsewhere insists.

Now what is the general result of this little study, the general impression that it leaves upon the mind? Certainly we feel that the life reflected in these sentences was a life in which caution was above all things necessary—caution in thought and speech and act, never ceasing, by night or day, during the whole of a man's life. Caution implies moderation. Moderation inevitably develops a certain habit of justice—a justice that might not extend outside of the race, but a justice that would be exercised between man and man of the same blood. Very much of English character and of English history is explained by the life that the "Havamal" portrays. Very much that is good; also very much that is bad—not bad in one sense, so far as the future of the race is concerned, but in a social way certainly not good. The judgment of the Englishman by all other European peoples is that he is the most suspicious, the most reserved, the most unreceptive, the most unfriendly, the coldest hearted, and the most domineering of all Western peoples. Ask a Frenchman, an Italian, a German, a Spaniard, even an American, what he thinks about Englishmen; and every one of them will tell you the very same thing. This is precisely what the character of men would become who had lived for thousands of years in the conditions of Northern society. But you would find upon the other hand that nearly all nations would speak highly of certain other English qualities—energy, courage, honour, justice (between themselves). They would say that although no man is so difficult to make friends with, the friendship of an

Englishman once gained is more strong and true than any other. And as the battle of life still continues, and must continue for thousands of years to come, it must be acknowledged that the English character is especially well fitted for the struggle. Its reserves, its cautions, its doubts, its suspicions, its brutality—these have been for it in the past, and are still in the present, the best social armour and panoply of war. It is not a lovable nor an amiable character; it is not even kindly. The Englishman of the best type is much more inclined to be just than he is to be kind, for kindness is an emotional impulse, and the Englishman is on his guard against every kind of emotional impulse. But with all this, the character is a grand one, and its success has been the best proof of its value.

Now you will have observed in the reading of this ancient code of social morals that, while none of the teaching is religious, some of it is absolutely immoral from any religious standpoint. No great religion permits us to speak what is not true, and to smile in the face of an enemy while pretending to be his friend. No religion teaches that we should "pay back lies for lies." Neither does a religion tell us that we should expect a return for every kindness done; that we should regard friendship as being actuated by selfish motives; that we should never praise when praise seems to be deserved. In fact, when Sir Walter Scott long ago made a partial translation of the "Havamal," he thought himself obliged to leave out a number of sentences which seemed to him highly immoral, and to apologize for others. He thought that they would shock English readers too much.

We are not quite so squeamish to-day; and a thinker of our own time would scarcely deny that English society is very largely governed at this moment by the same kind of rules that Sir Walter Scott thought to be so bad. But here we need not condemn English society in particular. All European society has been for hundreds of years conducting itself upon very much the same principles; for the reason that human social experience has been the same in all Western countries. I should say that the only difference between English society and other societies is that the hardness of character is very much greater. Let us go back even to the most Christian times of Western societies in the most Christian country of Europe, and observe whether the social code was then and there so very different from the social code of the old "Havamal." Mr. Spencer observes in his "Ethics" that, so far as the conduct of life is concerned, religion is almost nothing and practice is everything. We find this wonderfully exemplified in a most remarkable book of social precepts written in the seventeenth century, in Spain, under the title of the "Oraculo Manual." It was composed by a Spanish priest, named Baltasar Gracian, who was born in the year 1601 and died in 1658; and it has been translated into nearly all languages. The best English translation, published by Macmillan, is called "The Art of Worldly Wisdom." It is even more admired to-day than in the seventeenth century; and what it teaches as to social conduct holds as good to-day of modern society as it did of society two hundred years ago. It is one of the most unpleasant and yet interesting books ever published—unpleasant because of the malicious cunning which it often displays—interesting because of the frightful perspicacity of the author. The man who wrote that book understood the hearts of men, especially the bad side. He was a gentleman of high rank before he became a priest, and his instinctive shrewdness must have been hereditary. Religion, this man would have said, teaches the best possible morals; but the world is not governed by religion altogether, and to mix with it, we must act according to its dictates.

These dictates remind us in many ways of the cautions and the cunning of the "Havamal." The first thing enjoined upon a man both by the Norse writer and by the Spanish author is the art of silence. Probably this has been the result of social experience in all countries. "Cautious silence is the holy of holies of worldly wisdom," says Gracian. And he gives many elaborate reasons for this statement, not the least of which is the following: "If you do not declare yourself immediately, you arouse expectation, especially when the importance of your position makes you the object of general attention. Mix a little mystery with everything, and the very mystery arouses veneration." A little further on he gives us exactly the same advice as did the "Havamal" writer, in regard to being frank with enemies. "Do not," he says, "show your wounded finger, for everything will knock up against it; nor complain about it, for malice always aims where weakness can be injured. . . . Never disclose the source of mortification or of joy, if you wish the one to cease, the other to endure." About secrets the Spaniard is quite as cautious as the Norseman. He says, "Especially dangerous are secrets entrusted to friends. He that communicates his secret to another makes himself that other man's slave." But after a great many such cautions in regard to silence and secrecy, he tells us also that we must learn how to fight with the world. You remember the advice of the "Havamal" on this subject, how it condemns as a fool the man who can not answer a reproach. The Spaniard is, however, much more malicious in his suggestions. He tells us that we must "learn to know every man's thumbscrew." I suppose you know that a thumbscrew was an instrument of torture used in old times to force confessions from criminals. This advice means nothing less than that we should learn how to be able to hurt other men's feelings, or to flatter other men's weaknesses. "First guess every man's ruling passion, appeal to it by a word, set it in motion by temptation, and you will infallibly give checkmate to his freedom of will." The term "give checkmate" is taken from the game of chess, and must here be understood as meaning to overcome, to conquer. A kindred piece of advice is "keep a store of sarcasms, and know how to use them." Indeed he tells us that this is the point of greatest tact in human intercourse. "Struck by the slightest word of this kind, many fall away from the closest intimacy with superiors or inferiors, which intimacy could not be in the slightest shaken by a whole conspiracy of popular insinuation or private malevolence." In other words, you can more quickly destroy a man's friendship by one word of sarcasm than by any amount of intrigue. Does not this read very much like sheer wickedness? Certainly it does; but the author would have told you that you must fight the wicked with their own weapons. In the "Havamal" you will not find anything quite so openly wicked as that; but we must suppose that the Norsemen knew the secret, though they might not have put it into words. As for the social teaching, you will find it very subtly expressed even in the modern English novels of George Meredith, who, by the way, has written a poem in praise of sarcasm and ridicule. But let us now see what the Spanish author has to tell us about friendship and unselfishness.

The shrewd man knows that others when they seek him do not seek "him," but "their advantage in him and by him." That is to say, a shrewd man does not believe in disinterested friendship. This is much worse than anything in the "Havamal." And it is diabolically elaborated. What are we to say about such teaching as the following: "A wise man would rather see men needing him than thanking him. To keep them on the threshold of hope is diplomatic; to trust to their gratitude is boorish; hope has a good memory, gratitude a bad one"?

There is much more of this kind; but after the assurance that only a boorish person (that is to say, an ignorant and vulgar man) can believe in gratitude, the author's opinion of human nature needs no further elucidation. The old Norseman would have been shocked at such a statement. But he might have approved the following: "When you hear anything favourable, keep a tight rein upon your credulity; if unfavourable, give it the spur." That is to say, when you hear anything good about another man, do not be ready to believe it; but if you hear anything bad about him, believe as much of it as you can.

I notice also many other points of resemblance between the Northern and the Spanish teaching in regard to caution. The "Havamal" says that you must not pick a quarrel with a worse man than yourself; "because the better man often falls by the worse man's sword." The Spanish priest gives a still shrewder reason for the same policy. "Never contend," he says, "with a man who has nothing to lose; for thereby you enter into an unequal conflict. The other enters without anxiety; having lost everything, including shame, he has no further loss to fear." I think that this is an immoral teaching, though a very prudent one; but I need scarcely to tell you that it is still a principle in modern society not to contend with a man who has no reputation to lose. I think it is immoral, because it is purely selfish, and because a good man ought not to be afraid to denounce a wrong because of making enemies. Another point, however, on which the "Havamal" and the priest agree, is more commendable and interesting. "We do not think much of a man who never contradicts us; that is no sign he loves us, but rather a sign that he loves himself. Original and out-of-the way views are signs of superior ability."

I should not like you to suppose, however, that the whole of the book from which I have been quoting is of the same character as the quotations. There is excellent advice in it; and much kindly teaching on the subject of generous acts. It is a book both good and bad, and never stupid. The same man who tells you that friendship is seldom unselfish, also declares that life would be a desert without friends, and that there is no magic like a good turn—that is, a kind act. He teaches the importance of getting good will by honest means, although he advises us also to learn how to injure. I am sure that nobody could read the book without benefit. And I may close these quotations from it with the following paragraph, which is the very best bit of counsel that could be given to a literary student:

Be slow and sure. Quickly done can be quickly undone. To last an eternity requires an eternity of preparation. Only excellence counts. Profound intelligence is the only foundation for immortality. Worth much costs much. The precious metals are the heaviest.

But so far as the question of human conduct is concerned, the book of Gracian is no more of a religious book than is the "Havamal" of the heathen North. You would find, were such a book published to-day and brought up to the present time by any shrewd writer, that Western morality has not improved in the least since the time before Christianity was established, so far as the rules of society go. Society is not, and can not be, religious, because it is a state of continual warfare. Every person in it has to fight, and the battle is not less cruel now because it is not fought with swords. Indeed, I should think that the time when every man carried his sword in society was a time when men were quite as kindly and much more honest than they are now.

The object of this little lecture was to show you that the principles of the ancient Norse are really the principles ruling English society to-day; but I think you will be able to take from it a still larger meaning. It is that not only one form of society, but all forms of society, represent the warfare of man and man. That is why thinkers, poets, philosophers, in all ages, have tried to find solitude, to keep out of the contest, to devote themselves only to study of the beautiful and the true. But the prizes of life are not to be obtained in solitude, although the prizes of thought can only there be won. After all, whatever we may think about the cruelty and treachery of the social world, it does great things in the end. It quickens judgment, deepens intelligence, enforces the acquisition of self-control, creates forms of mental and moral strength that cannot fail to be sometimes of vast importance to mankind. But if you should ask me whether it increases human happiness, I should certainly say "no." The

"Havamal" said the same thing,—**the truly wise man cannot be happy."**

The Havamal[40]

Wisdom for Wanderers and Counsel to Guests

1.

At every door-way,
ere one enters,
one should spy round,
one should pry round
for uncertain is the witting
that there be no foeman sitting,
within, before one on the floor

2.

Hail, ye Givers! a guest is come;
say! where shall he sit within?
Much pressed is he who fain on the
hearth
would seek for warmth and weal.

Figure 98 - "The Stranger at the Door"
(1908) by W. G. Collingwood.

3.

He hath need of fire, who now is
come,
numbed with cold to the knee;
food and clothing the wanderer
craves
who has fared o'er the rimy fell.

4.

He craves for water, who comes for refreshment,
drying and friendly bidding,
marks of good will, fair fame if 'tis won,
and welcome once and again.

5.

He hath need of his wits who wanders wide,
aught simple will serve at home;

---

[40] as translated by Oliver Bray in 1908

but a gazing-stock is the fool who sits
mid the wise, and nothing knows.

6.
Let no man glory in the greatness of his mind,
but rather keep watch o'er his wits.
Cautious and silent let him enter a dwelling;
to the heedful comes seldom harm,
for none can find a more faithful friend
than the wealth of mother wit.

7.
Let the wary stranger who seeks refreshment
keep silent with sharpened hearing;
with his ears let him listen, and look with his eyes;
thus each wise man spies out the way.

8.
Happy is he who wins for himself
fair fame and kindly words;
but uneasy is that which a man doth own
while it lies in another's breast.

9.
Happy is he who hath in himself
praise and wisdom in life;
for oft doth a man ill counsel get
when 'tis born in another's breast.

10.
A better burden can no man bear
on the way than his mother wit;
'tis the refuge of the poor, and richer it seems
than wealth in a world untried.

11.
A better burden can no man bear
on the way than his mother wit:
and no worse provision can he carry with him
than too deep a draught of ale.

12.
Less good than they say for the sons of men
is the drinking oft of ale:
for the more they drink, the less can they think
and keep a watch o'er their wits.

13.
A bird of Unmindfulness flutters o'er ale feasts,
wiling away men's wits:
with the feathers of that fowl I was fettered once
in the garths of Gunnlos below.

14.
Drunk was I then, I was over drunk
in that crafty Jötun's court.
But best is an ale feast when man is able
to call back his wits at once.

15.
Silent and thoughtful and bold in strife
the prince's bairn should be.
Joyous and generous let each man show him
until he shall suffer death.

16.
A coward believes he will ever live
if he keep him safe from strife:
but old age leaves him not long in peace
though spears may spare his life.

17.
A fool will gape when he goes to a friend,
and mumble only, or mope;
but pass him the ale cup and all in a moment
the mind of that man is shown.

18.
He knows alone who has wandered wide,
and far has fared on the way,

what manner of mind a man doth own
who is wise of head and heart.

19.
Keep not the mead cup but drink thy measure;
speak needful words or none:
none shall upbraid thee for lack of breeding
if soon thou seek'st thy rest.

20.
A greedy man, if he be not mindful,
eats to his own life's hurt:
oft the belly of the fool will bring him to scorn
when he seeks the circle of the wise.

21.
Herds know the hour of their going home
and turn them again from the grass;
but never is found a foolish man
who knows the measure of his maw.

22.
The miserable man and evil minded
makes of all things mockery,
and knows not that which he best should know,
that he is not free from faults.

23.
The unwise man is awake all night,
and ponders everything over;
when morning comes he is weary in mind,
and all is a burden as ever.

24.
The unwise man weens all who smile
and flatter him are his friends,
nor notes how oft they speak him ill
when he sits in the circle of the wise.

25.
The unwise man weens all who smile
and flatter him are his friends;
but when he shall come into court he shall find
there are few to defend his cause.

26.
The unwise man thinks all to know,
while he sits in a sheltered nook;
but he knows not one thing, what he shall answer,
if men shall put him to proof.

27.
For the unwise man 'tis best to be mute
when he come amid the crowd,
for none is aware of his lack of wit
if he wastes not too many words;
for he who lacks wit shall never learn
though his words flow ne'er so fast.

28.
Wise he is deemed who can question well,
and also answer back:
the sons of men can no secret make
of the tidings told in their midst.

29.
Too many unstable words are spoken
by him who ne'er holds his peace;
the hasty tongue sings its own mishap
if it be not bridled in.

30.
Let no man be held as a laughing-stock,
though he come as guest for a meal:
wise enough seem many while they sit dry-skinned
and are not put to proof.

31.
A guest thinks him witty who mocks at a guest

and runs from his wrath away;
but none can be sure who jests at a meal
that he makes not fun among foes.

32.
Oft, though their hearts lean towards one another,
friends are divided at table;
ever the source of strife 'twill be,
that guest will anger guest.

33.
A man should take always his meals betimes
unless he visit a friend,
or he sits and mopes, and half famished seems,
and can ask or answer nought.

34.
Long is the round to a false friend leading,
e'en if he dwell on the way:
but though far off fared, to a faithful friend
straight are the roads and short.

35.
A guest must depart again on his way,
nor stay in the same place ever;
if he bide too long on another's bench
the loved one soon becomes loathed.

36.
One's own house is best, though small it may be;
each man is master at home;
though he have but two goats and a bark-thatched hut
'tis better than craving a boon.

37.
One's own house is best, though small it may be,
each man is master at home;
with a bleeding heart will he beg, who must,
his meat at every meal.

38.
Let a man never stir on his road a step
without his weapons of war;
for unsure is the knowing when need shall arise
of a spear on the way without.

39.
I found none so noble or free with his food,
who was not gladdened with a gift,
nor one who gave of his gifts such store
but he loved reward, could he win it.

40.
Let no man stint him and suffer need
of the wealth he has won in life;
oft is saved for a foe what was meant for a friend,
and much goes worse than one weens.

41.
With raiment and arms shall friends gladden each other,
so has one proved oneself;
for friends last longest, if fate be fair
who give and give again.

42.
To his friend a man should bear him as friend,
and gift for gift bestow,
laughter for laughter let him exchange,
but leasing pay for a lie.

43.
To his friend a man should bear him as friend,
to him and a friend of his;
but let him beware that he be not the friend
of one who is friend to his foe.

44.
Hast thou a friend whom thou trustest well,
from whom thou cravest good?

Share thy mind with him, gifts exchange with him,
fare to find him oft.

45.
But hast thou one whom thou trustest ill
yet from whom thou cravest good?
Thou shalt speak him fair, but falsely think,
and leasing pay for a lie.

46.
Yet further of him whom thou trusted ill,
and whose mind thou dost misdoubt;
thou shalt laugh with him but withhold thy thought,
for gift with like gift should be paid.

47.
Young was I once, I walked alone,
and bewildered seemed in the way;
then I found me another and rich I thought me,
for man is the joy of man.

48.
Most blest is he who lives free and bold
and nurses never a grief,
for the fearful man is dismayed by aught,
and the mean one mourns over giving.

49.
My garments once I gave in the field
to two land-marks made as men;
heroes they seemed when once they were clothed;
'tis the naked who suffer shame!

50.
The pine tree wastes which is perched on the hill,
nor bark nor needles shelter it;
such is the man whom none doth love;
for what should he longer live?

51.
Fiercer than fire among ill friends
for five days love will burn;
bun anon 'tis quenched, when the sixth day comes,
and all friendship soon is spoiled.

52.
Not great things alone must one give to another,
praise oft is earned for nought;
with half a loaf and a tilted bowl
I have found me many a friend.

53.
Little the sand if little the seas,
little are minds of men,
for ne'er in the world were all equally wise,
'tis shared by the fools and the sage.

54.
Wise in measure let each man be;
but let him not wax too wise;
for never the happiest of men is he
who knows much of many things.

55.
Wise in measure should each man be;
but let him not wax too wise;
seldom a heart will sing with joy
if the owner be all too wise.

56.
Wise in measure should each man be,
but ne'er let him wax too wise:
who looks not forward to learn his fate
unburdened heart will bear.

57.
Brand kindles from brand until it be burned,
spark is kindled from spark,

man unfolds him by speech with man,
but grows over secret through silence.

58.
He must rise betimes who fain of another
or life or wealth would win;
scarce falls the prey to sleeping wolves,
or to slumberers victory in strife.

59.
He must rise betimes who hath few to serve him,
and see to his work himself;
who sleeps at morning is hindered much,
to the keen is wealth half-won.

60.
Of dry logs saved and roof-bark stored
a man can know the measure,
of fire-wood too which should last him out
quarter and half years to come.

61.
Fed and washed should one ride to court
though in garments none too new;
thou shalt not shame thee for shoes or breeks,
nor yet for a sorry steed.

62.
Like an eagle swooping over old ocean,
snatching after his prey,
so comes a man into court who finds
there are few to defend his cause.

63.
Each man who is wise and would wise be called
must ask and answer aright.
Let one know thy secret, but never a second,
if three a thousand shall know.

64.
A wise counselled man will be mild in bearing
and use his might in measure,
lest when he come his fierce foes among
he find others fiercer than he.

65.
Each man should be watchful and wary in speech,
and slow to put faith in a friend.
for the words which one to another speaks
he may win reward of ill.

66.
At many a feast I was far too late,
and much too soon at some;
drunk was the ale or yet unserved:
never hits he the joint who is hated.

67.
Here and there to a home I had haply been asked
had I needed no meat at my meals,
or were two hams left hanging in the house of that friend
where I had partaken of one.

68.
Most dear is fire to the sons of men,
most sweet the sight of the sun;
good is health if one can but keep it,
and to live a life without shame.

69.
Not reft of all is he who is ill,
for some are blest in their bairns,
some in their kin and some in their wealth,
and some in working well.

70.
More blest are the living than the lifeless,
'tis the living who come by the cow;

I saw the hearth-fire burn in the rich man's hall
and himself lying dead at the door.

71.
The lame can ride horse, the handless drive cattle,
the deaf one can fight and prevail,
'tis happier for the blind than for him on the bale-fire,
but no man hath care for a corpse.

72.
Best have a son though he be late born
and before him the father be dead:
seldom are stones on the wayside raised
save by kinsmen to kinsmen.

73.
Two are hosts against one, the tongue is the head's bane,
'neath a rough hide a hand may be hid;
he is glad at nightfall who knows of his lodging,
short is the ship's berth,
and changeful the autumn night,
much veers the wind ere the fifth day
and blows round yet more in a month.

74.
He that learns nought will never know
how one is the fool of another,
for if one be rich another is poor
and for that should bear no blame.

75.
Cattle die and kinsmen die,
thyself too soon must die,
but one thing never, I ween, will die,
fair fame of one who has earned.

76.
Cattle die and kinsmen die,
thyself too soon must die,

but one thing never, I ween, will die,
the doom on each one dead.

77.
Full-stocked folds had the Fatling's sons,
who bear now a beggar's staff:
brief is wealth, as the winking of an eye,
most faithless ever of friends.

78.
If haply a fool should find for himself
wealth or a woman's love,
pride waxes in him but wisdom never
and onward he fares in his folly.

79.
All will prove true that thou askest of runes
those that are come from the gods,
which the high Powers wrought, and which Odin painted:
then silence is surely best.

Maxims for All Men

80.
Praise day at even, a wife when dead,
a weapon when tried, a maid when married,
ice when 'tis crossed, and ale when 'tis drunk.

81.
Hew wood in wind, sail the seas in a breeze,
woo a maid in the dark, -- for day's eyes are many,
work a ship for its gliding, a shield for its shelter,
a sword for its striking, a maid for her kiss;

82.
Drink ale by the fire, but slide on the ice;
buy a steed when 'tis lanky, a sword when 'tis rusty;
feed thy horse neath a roof, and thy hound in the yard.

83.
The speech of a maiden should no man trust
nor the words which a woman says;
for their hearts were shaped on a whirling wheel
and falsehood fixed in their breasts.

84.
Breaking bow, or flaring flame,
ravening wolf, or croaking raven,
routing swine, or rootless tree,
waxing wave, or seething cauldron,

85.
flying arrows, or falling billow,
ice of a nighttime, coiling adder,
woman's bed-talk, or broken blade,
play of bears or a prince's child,

86.
sickly calf or self-willed thrall,
witch's flattery, new-slain foe,
brother's slayer, though seen on the highway,

half burned house, or horse too swift
be never so trustful as these to trust.

87.
Let none put faith in the first sown fruit
nor yet in his son too soon;
whim rules the child, and weather the field,
each is open to chance.

88.
Like the love of women whose thoughts are lies
is the driving un-roughshod o'er slippery ice
of a two year old, ill-tamed and gay;
or in a wild wind steering a helmless ship,
or the lame catching reindeer in the rime-thawed fell.

Lessons for Lovers

89.
Now plainly I speak, since both I have seen;
unfaithful is man to maid;
we speak them fairest when thoughts are falsest
and wile the wisest of hearts.

90.
Let him speak soft words and offer wealth
who longs for a woman's love,
praise the shape of the shining maid
he wins who thus doth woo.

91.
-- Never a whit should one blame another
whom love hath brought into bonds:
oft a witching form will fetch the wise
which holds not the heart of fools.

92.
Never a whit should one blame another
for a folly which many befalls;

the might of love makes sons of men
into fools who once were wise.

93.
The mind knows alone what is nearest the heart
and sees where the soul is turned:
no sickness seems to the wise so sore
as in nought to know content.

Odin's Love Quests

94.
This once I felt when I sat without
in the reeds, and looked for my love;
body and soul of me was that sweet maiden
yet never I won her as wife.

95.
Billing's daughter I found on her bed,
fairer than sunlight sleeping,
and the sweets of lordship seemed to me nought,
save I lived with that lovely form.

96.
"Yet nearer evening come thou, Odin,
if thou wilt woo a maiden:
all were undone save two knew alone
such a secret deed of shame."

97.
So away I turned from my wise intent,
and deemed my joy assured,
for all her liking and all her love
I weened that I yet should win.

98.
When I came ere long the war troop bold
were watching and waking all:
with burning brands and torches borne
they showed me my sorrowful way.

99.
Yet nearer morning I went, once more,
the housefolk slept in the hall,
but soon I found a barking dog
tied fast to that fair maid's couch.

100.
Many a sweet maid when one knows her mind

is fickle found towards men:
I proved it well when that prudent lass
I sought to lead astray:
shrewd maid, she sought me with every insult
and I won therewith no wife.

Odin's Quest after the Song Mead

101.
In thy home be joyous and generous to guests
discreet shalt thou be in thy bearing,
mindful and talkative, wouldst thou gain wisdom,
oft making me mention of good.
He is "Simpleton" named who has nought to say,
for such is the fashion of fools.

102.
I sought that old Jötun, now safe am I back,
little served my silence there;
but whispering many soft speeches I won
my desire in Suttung's halls.

103.
I bored me a road there with Rati's tusk
and made room to pass through the rock;
while the ways of the Jötuns stretched over and under,
I dared my life for a draught.

104.
'Twas Gunnlod who gave me on a golden throne
a draught of the glorious mead,
but with poor reward did I pay her back
for her true and troubled heart.

105.
In a wily disguise I worked my will;
little is lacking to the wise,
for the Soul-stirrer now, sweet Mead of Song,
is brought to men's earthly abode.

106.
I misdoubt me if ever again I had come
from the realms of the Jötun race,
had I not served me of Gunnlod, sweet woman,
her whom I held in mine arms.

107.
Came forth, next day, the dread Frost Giants,
and entered the High One's Hall:
they asked -- was the Baleworker back mid the Powers,
or had Suttung slain him below?

108.
A ring-oath Odin I trow had taken
how shall one trust his troth?
'twas he who stole the mead from Suttung,
and Gunnlod caused to weep.

The Counseling of the Stray-Singer

109.
'Tis time to speak from the Sage's Seat;
hard by the Well of Weird
I saw and was silent, I saw and pondered,
I listened to the speech of men.

110.
Of runes they spoke, and the reading of runes
was little withheld from their lips:
at the High One's hall, in the High One's hall,
I thus heard the High One say: --

111.
I counsel thee, Stray-Singer, accept my counsels,
they will be thy boon if thou obey'st them,
they will work thy weal if thou win'st them:
rise never at nighttime, except thou art spying
or seekest a spot without.

112.
I counsel thee, Stray-Singer, accept my counsels,
they will be thy boon if thou obey'st them,
they will work thy weal if thou win'st them:
thou shalt never sleep in the arms of a sorceress,
lest she should lock thy limbs;

113.
So shall she charm that thou shalt not heed
the council, or words of the king,
nor care for thy food, or the joys of mankind,
but fall into sorrowful sleep.

114.
I counsel thee, Stray-Singer, accept my counsels,
they will be thy boon if thou obey'st them,
they will work thy weal if thou win'st them:
seek not ever to draw to thyself
in love-whispering another's wife.

115.
I counsel thee, Stray-Singer, accept my counsels,
they will be thy boon if thou obey'st them,
they will work thy weal if thou win'st them:
should thou long to fare over fell and firth
provide thee well with food.

116.
I counsel thee, Stray-Singer, accept my counsels,
they will be thy boon if thou obey'st them,
they will work thy weal if thou win'st them:
tell not ever an evil man
if misfortunes thee befall,
from such ill friend thou needst never seek
return for thy trustful mind.

117.
Wounded to death, have I seen a man
by the words of an evil woman;

a lying tongue had bereft him of life,
and all without reason of right.

118.
I counsel thee, Stray-Singer, accept my counsels,
they will be thy boon if thou obey'st them,
they will work thy weal if thou win'st them:
hast thou a friend whom thou trustest well,
fare thou to find him oft;
for with brushwood grows and with grasses high
the path where no foot doth pass.

119.
I counsel thee, Stray-Singer, accept my counsels,
they will be thy boon if thou obey'st them,
they will work thy weal if thou win'st them:
in sweet converse call the righteous to thy side,
learn a healing song while thou livest.

120.
I counsel thee, Stray-Singer, accept my counsels,
they will be thy boon if thou obey'st them,
they will work thy weal if thou win'st them:
be never the first with friend of thine
to break the bond of fellowship;
care shall gnaw thy heart if thou canst not tell
all thy mind to another.

121.
I counsel thee, Stray-Singer, accept my counsels,
they will be thy boon if thou obey'st them,
they will work thy weal if thou win'st them:
never in speech with a foolish knave
shouldst thou waste a single word.

122.
From the lips of such thou needst not look
for reward of thine own good will;
but a righteous man by praise will render thee
firm in favour and love.

123.
There is mingling in friendship when man can utter
all his whole mind to another;
there is nought so vile as a fickle tongue;
no friend is he who but flatters.

124.
I counsel thee, Stray-Singer, accept my counsels,
they will be thy boon if thou obey'st them,
they will work thy weal if thou win'st them:
oft the worst lays the best one low.

125.
I counsel thee, Stray-Singer, accept my counsels,
they will be thy boon if thou obey'st them,
they will work thy weal if thou win'st them:
be not a shoemaker nor yet a shaft maker
save for thyself alone:
let the shoe be misshapen, or crooked the shaft,
and a curse on thy head will be called.

126.
I counsel thee, Stray-Singer, accept my counsels,
they will be thy boon if thou obey'st them,
they will work thy weal if thou win'st them:
when in peril thou seest thee, confess thee in peril,
nor ever give peace to thy foes.

127.
I counsel thee, Stray-Singer, accept my counsels,
they will be thy boon if thou obey'st them,
they will work thy weal if thou win'st them:
rejoice not ever at tidings of ill,
but glad let thy soul be in good.

128.
I counsel thee, Stray-Singer, accept my counsels,
they will be thy boon if thou obey'st them,
they will work thy weal if thou win'st them:

look not up in battle, when men are as beasts,
lest the wights bewitch thee with spells.

129.
I counsel thee, Stray-Singer, accept my counsels,
they will be thy boon if thou obey'st them,
they will work thy weal if thou win'st them:
wouldst thou win joy of a gentle maiden,
and lure to whispering of love,
thou shalt make fair promise, and let it be fast,
none will scorn their weal who can win it.

130.
I counsel thee, Stray-Singer, accept my counsels,
they will be thy boon if thou obey'st them,
they will work thy weal if thou win'st them:
I pray thee be wary, yet not too wary,
be wariest of all with ale,
with another's wife, and a third thing eke,
that knaves outwit thee never.

131.
I counsel thee, Stray-Singer, accept my counsels,
they will be thy boon if thou obey'st them,
they will work thy weal if thou win'st them:
hold not in scorn, nor mock in thy halls
a guest or wandering wight.

132.
They know but unsurely who sit within
what manner of man is come:
none is found so good, but some fault attends him,
or so ill but he serves for somewhat.

133.
I counsel thee, Stray-Singer, accept my counsels,
they will be thy boon if thou obey'st them,
they will work thy weal if thou win'st them:
hold never in scorn the hoary singer;
oft the counsel of the old is good;

come words of wisdom from the withered lips
of him left to hang among hides,
to rock with the rennets
and swing with the skins.

134.
I counsel thee, Stray-Singer, accept my counsels,
they will be thy boon if thou obey'st them,
they will work thy weal if thou win'st them:
growl not at guests, nor drive them from the gate
but show thyself gentle to the poor.

135.
Mighty is the bar to be moved away
for the entering in of all.
Shower thy wealth, or men shall wish thee
every ill in thy limbs.

136.
I counsel thee, Stray-Singer, accept my counsels,
they will be thy boon if thou obey'st them,
they will work thy weal if thou win'st them:
when ale thou quaffest, call upon earth's might --
'tis earth drinks in the floods.
Earth prevails o'er drink, but fire o'er sickness,
the oak o'er binding, the earcorn o'er witchcraft,
the rye spur o'er rupture, the moon o'er rages,
herb o'er cattle plagues, runes o'er harm.

Odin's Quest after the Runes

137.
I know I hung on that windy Tree
nine whole days and nights,
stabbed with a spear, offered to Odin,
myself to mine own self given,
high on that Tree of which none hath heard
from what roots it rises to heaven.

138.
None refreshed me ever with food or drink,
I peered right down in the deep;
crying aloud I lifted the Runes
then back I fell from thence.

139.
Nine mighty songs I learned
from the great
son of Bale-thorn, Bestla's
sire;
I drank a measure of the
wondrous Mead,
with the Soulstirrer's drops I
was showered.

140.
Ere long I bare fruit, and
throve full well,
I grew and waxed in
wisdom;
word following word, I
found me words,
deed following deed, I
wrought deeds.

141.
Hidden Runes shalt thou seek and interpreted signs,
many symbols of might and power,
by the great Singer
painted, by the high
Powers fashioned,
graved by the Utterer of
gods.

Figure 99 - "Odin's Self-sacrifice" (1908) by W. G.
Collingwood.

142.
For gods graved Odin, for elves graved Daïn,
Dvalin the Dallier for dwarfs,
All-wise for Jötuns, and I, of myself,
graved some for the sons of men.

143.
Dost know how to write, dost know how to read,
dost know how to paint, dost know how to prove,
dost know how to ask, dost know how to offer,
dost know how to send, dost know how to spend?

144.
Better ask for too little than offer too much,
like the gift should be the boon;
better not to send than to overspend.
....
Thus Odin graved ere the world began;
Then he rose from the deep, and came again.

The Song of Spells[41]

145.
Those songs I know, which nor sons of men
nor queen in a king's court knows;
the first is Help which will bring thee help
in all woes and in sorrow and strife.

146.
A second I know, which the son of men
must sing, who would heal the sick.

147.
A third I know: if sore need should come
of a spell to stay my foes;
when I sing that song, which shall blunt their swords,
nor their weapons nor Stáves can wound.

148.
A fourth I know: if men make fast
in chains the joints of my limbs,

---

[41] The following 18 verses are "spells" and are related to Galdr, or chanted incantations.

when I sing that song which shall set me free,
spring the fetters from hands and feet.

149.
A fifth I know: when I see, by foes shot,
speeding a shaft through the host,
flies it never so strongly I still can stay it,
if I get but a glimpse of its flight.

150.
A sixth I know: when some thane would harm me
in runes on a moist tree's root,
on his head alone shall light the ills
of the curse that he called upon mine.

151.
A seventh I know: if I see a hall
high o'er the bench-mates blazing,
flame it ne'er so fiercely I still can save it,
I know how to sing that song.

152.
An eighth I know: which all can sing
for their weal if they learn it well;
where hate shall wax 'mid the warrior sons,
I can calm it soon with that song.

153.
A ninth I know: when need befalls me
to save my vessel afloat,
I hush the wind on the stormy wave,
and soothe all the sea to rest.

154.
A tenth I know: when at night the witches
ride and sport in the air,
such spells I weave that they wander home
out of skins and wits bewildered.

155.
An eleventh I know: if haply I lead
my old comrades out to war,
I sing 'neath the shields, and they fare forth mightily
safe into battle,
safe out of battle,
and safe return from the strife.

156.
A twelfth I know: if I see in a tree
a corpse from a halter hanging,
such spells I write, and paint in runes,
that the being descends and speaks.

157.
A thirteenth I know: if the new-born son
of a warrior I sprinkle with water,
that youth will not fail when he fares to war,
never slain shall he bow before sword.

158.
A fourteenth I know: if I needs must number
the Powers to the people of men,
I know all the nature of gods and of elves
which none can know untaught.

159.
A fifteenth I know, which Folk-stirrer sang,
the dwarf, at the gates of Dawn;
he sang strength to the gods, and skill to the elves,
and wisdom to Odin who utters.

160.
A sixteenth I know: when all sweetness and love
I would win from some artful wench,
her heart I turn, and the whole mind change
of that fair-armed lady I love.

161.
A seventeenth I know: so that e'en the shy maiden
is slow to shun my love.

162.
These songs, Stray-Singer, which man's son knows not,
long shalt thou lack in life,
though thy weal if thou win'st them, thy boon if thou obey'st them
thy good if haply thou gain'st them.

163.
An eighteenth I know: which I ne'er shall tell
to maiden or wife of man
save alone to my sister, or haply to her
who folds me fast in her arms;
most safe are secrets known to but one-
the songs are sung to an end.

164.
Now the sayings of the High One are uttered in the hall
for the weal of men, for the woe of Jötuns,
Hail, thou who hast spoken! Hail, thou that knowest!
Hail, ye that have hearkened! Use, thou who hast learned!

Chapter 9 – Spiritual Practices

 ur forefathers had a complex, and sophisticated tradition relating to the spiritual aspects of life; in addition to the pantheon of deities discussed previously, they practiced methods to divine the future and make decisions, connect with the spirits in the other worlds, and take journeys beyond the realm of Midgard.

In this chapter we'll explore esoteric uses of the Runes - Runic Divination. I'll also briefly introduce you to a method to contact your Fylgia – or spirit guide.

Much of what we'll cover in this chapter has been re-created in modern times, with inspiration from documented practices of the North, and borrowing some bits and pieces from other cultures. As we established at the beginning of our journey, our Lore is a living organism which evolves over time. You too will influence the evolution of that lore.

Runic Divination

Evolution

There is evidence that runes historically served purposes of magic in addition to being a writing system. This is the case from earliest epigraphic evidence of the Roman to Germanic Iron Age, and in medieval sources, notably the Poetic Edda. The Sigrdrífumál mentions "victory runes" to be carved on a sword, "some on the grasp and some on the inlay, and name Tyr twice."

Tacitus, the Roman historian, wrote the earliest known detailed description of Runic divination.

> *Their method of divining by lots is exceedingly simple. From a tree which bears fruit they cut a twig, and divide it into two small pieces. These they distinguish by so many several marks, and throw them at random and without order upon a white garment. Then the Priest of the community, if for the public the lots are consulted, or the father of a family about a private concern, after he has solemnly invoked the Gods, with eyes lifted up to heaven, takes up every piece thrice, and having done thus forms a judgment according to the marks before made.*
>
> - *Tacitus, Germania (98 CE)*

While there is no clear-cut evidence that the "marks" referred to by Tacitus were Runes, this would seem probable.

In the early 20th century, Germanic mysticism coins new forms of "runic magic", some of which were continued or developed further by contemporary adherents of Germanic Neopaganism. Modern systems of runic divination are based on Hermeticism[42] , classical Occultism, and the I Ching.

The Armanen runes "revealed" to Guido von List in 1902 were employed for magical purposes in Germanic mysticism by

---

[42] The term Hermetic is from the Greek word Herm, which refers to a pillar or post used in pre-classical Greece "of square shape, surmounted by a head with a beard. The square, limbless "Hermes" was a step in advance of the unwrought stone." The origin of the word Hermes relates to a stone pillar used to communicate with the deities and the use of names beginning with Herm in Greece dates from at least 600 BC. The God Hermes is a generic term used by the pre-classical Greeks for any deity, and was only later associated with the God of Knowledge in Athens in the 2nd Century AD. In Late Antiquity, Hermetism emerged in parallel with Gnosticism, Neoplatonism and early Christianity, "characterized by a resistance to the dominance of either pure rationality or doctrinal faith".

authors such as Friedrich Bernhard Marby and Siegfried Adolf Kummer, and after World War II in a reformed "pansophical " system by Karl Spiesberger. More recently, Stephen Flowers, Adolf Schleipfer, Larry E. Camp and others also build on List's system.

In 1982, the modern usage of the runes for answering life's questions was apparently originated by Ralph Blum in his divination book The Book of Runes: A Handbook for the Use of an Ancient Oracle, which was marketed with a small bag of round tiles with runes stamped on them. This book has remained in print since its first publication. The sources for Blum's divinatory interpretations, as he explained in The Book of Runes itself, drew heavily on then-current books describing the ancient I Ching divination system of China. Ralph Blum included the ahistorical "blank rune" in his 1982 book and rune set. In purchased sets, the blank rune may be used to replace any runes that are lost and should not to be included in a reading.

In the wake of a 1984 dissertation on "Runes and Magic", Stephen Flowers published a series of books under the pen-name "Edred Thorsson" which detailed his own original method of runic divination and magic, 'odianism', which he said was loosely based on historical sources and modern European hermeticism.

Use of the Elder Futhark

As we explored in Chapter 2 - Runes, there are many variants of the runic staves. In our exploration of the use of runes for divination, we'll work with the Elder Futhark; remember we've used the Elder Futhark in the Chapter 4 - Runic Yoga. Some may wonder why I chose the Elder, rather than the Younger, which has a more recent history, and more numerous extant inscriptions etc. There are a few reasons for my preference, and that's all it is, simply a preference. People around the world work successfully with all the families of runes, but the Elder Futhark seems to resonate with me.

We've already talked about how the runes are divided into groups called aetir – literally eights. The Elder Futhark are divided into three groups of eight runes; other families are grouped into three groups, but not necessarily of eight runes. To me this seems an inconsistency with the Elder Futhark. If our ancestors divided them into groups of eight, and we still use the term aetir, then why the change?

When contrasting the Elder versus Younger runic rows, I also noticed a significant difference in the scope of their interpretations that seemed to signify to me, a shift in the world view, or attitudes of our ancestors. For example the rune Kenaz in the Elder Futhark means Torch, and can symbolize light, learning and inspiration. It can also signify the energy of fire, in both negative and positive aspects. This description feels balanced to me. If we now look at the equivalent rune in the Younger Futhorc, Kaun, we see a marked difference in its meaning – Cancer, Ulcer. It seems to me to be a very negative rune. It's lost its balance in my view.

Other changes include the removal of Gebo, the rune for Gift, and of Wunjo, the rune for Joy. I'm speculating that perhaps due to the changes in conditions that drove our ancestors to go a-viking in the first place, they also began to have a more negative, and less balanced view of the world. In my own search for meaning, I'm looking for balance. To me, the Elder Futhark feels right. Let me add that I recognize that systems evolve, as the elder futhark did into the younger and others; perhaps for me choosing the elder runes, this is simply closing the loop on that evolution – coming full circle if you will.

Please don't let my preference dissuade you from using any of the different runic rows in your own work, I simply want to highlight my own rationale for choosing one over another.

Just a quick note, I will be using the commonly accepted reconstructed Germanic names for the runes.

How to use them

The most common way to use the runes today is the "drawing of lots" or picking runes to help guide us relating to some question. Typically a querent (the person with the question) will formulate the question, then draw runes from a bag. It could be a single rune, or several, as we'll see.

The runes themselves can be made out of many things as highlighted earlier. Occasionally their symbols are drawn on slips of paper – there are many sets of "rune cards" out there on the market. My personal belief is that the forces in the multiverse you are tapping into probably don't care what medium their counsel gets delivered on. I've even used computer generated rune readings with success.

"..remember to bear in mind that we are not playing at re-enactment, we are seiðrfolk living in the now and as such may feel free to use whatever tool we have around us that is most durable and best suited for our needs."

> *- Runic John (2004) – The Book of Seiðr (passage was discussing the use of organic versus man made paints)*

I have two sets of runes. The first set I made when I was first drawn to the runes and a more serious study of our Northern Lore - these were made from river stones. I carved the rune staves on them with a dremel rotary tool, and stained them with a mixture of ochre, boiled linseed oil and a few drops of my blood.

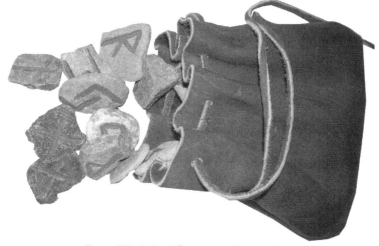

Figure 100 - Author's Runes carved on river stone

The set I use daily though, comes from the branch of an apple tree whose limb was broken during a storm. I carved slips of wood from the branch, then burned the runes onto each slip using a wood burning tool. I then coated them with boiled linseed oil. I also made a bag of pigskin, with a leather draw cord ending in a Boar's tusk. Yours needn't be as elaborate, but for me the joy in creating something beautiful, useful, and charged with so much meaning, was a spiritual practice in itself. One I am reminded of every time I take out my bag of runes.

Figure 101 - Author's Runes carved on slips of wood cut from an apple branch

Odin Cast

I often draw a single rune, sometimes referred to as an Odin cast, when I want some relatively straightforward guidance to a particular question and would go through the following steps:

1)   Relax your mind and ensure you are in a calm state and free from distractions and negative influences

2)   Formulate the question in your mind e.g. "What will happen if I take that new job?"

3)   Focus on the question as you **draw a single rune** - pick one you feel guided to

4)   Place the rune down on a table or other surface

5)   Interpret the possible meaning of the rune in relation to the question you have posed – consult the meanings and associations that follow

Norn Cast

A second method is used when you want more detailed guidance, and involves drawing three runes to provide a more complete picture of the influences on your question at hand. It is often referred to as a Norn cast, in reference to Urd, Verdandi and Skuld (representing past, present and future).

You would start the Norn cast in the same manner as the Odin cast, but would choose three runes, one at a time. Laying each down separately left to right. The first representing the past (Urd), the second representing the present (Verdandi),. And the final rune representing the future, or potential outcomes (Skuld).

Once the three runes were laid, you would then analyze the meaning of each. The first rune represents the forces or influences in your past, the second indicates condition or influences in your

present, and the third hints at potential outcomes and directions – our ancestors did not believe the future was pre-determined.

How to Interpret them

Each rune and it's meanings and associations have to be considered in the context of your life – which includes your past, present activity as well as considerations for the future.

Once you have drawn your rune(s), consult the descriptions of each rune. I've tried to provide the most common exoteric, as well as esoteric meanings associated with each rune (Per Thorsson, Aswynn, et al). Consider them carefully as you try to unlock the guidance you have been provided.

I've also provided the Anglo-Saxon rune poems for each. These may additionally have more subtle codified meanings for the runes.

"The Old English Rune Poem records stanzas for the twenty-nine-stave Old English Futhorc. This is especially valuable because it is a source for the lore of the staves of the Elder Futhark not present in the younger row."

- *Edred Thorsson, Futhark*

Name: Fehu
Meaning: Livestock, Wealth, Energy, Fertility, Creation
Phoenetic Value: F

Anglo–Saxon Rune Poem

Wealth is a comfort to all men,
Yet one must give it away freely,
If he wants to gain glory in the Lord's
sight.

Name: Uruz
Meaning: The Aurochs, Health, Wisdom, Vital Strength
Phoenetic Value: U

Anglo–Saxon Rune Poem

The aurochs is proud and has great horns;
* it is a very savage beast and fights with its*
horns;
* a great ranger of the moors, it is a creature of*
mettle.

Name: Thurisaz
Meaning: Giant, Thorn, Destruction/ Defense
Phoenetic Value: TH

Anglo–Saxon Rune Poem

The thorn is exceedingly sharp,
an evil thing for any knight to touch,
uncommonly severe on all who sit
among them.

Name: Ansuz
Meaning: A god (Odinn), Mouth, Song, Poetry, Inspiration, Knowledge
Phoenetic Value: A

Anglo–Saxon Rune Poem

The mouth is the source of all language,
a pillar of wisdom and a comfort to wise men,
a blessing and a joy to every knight.

281

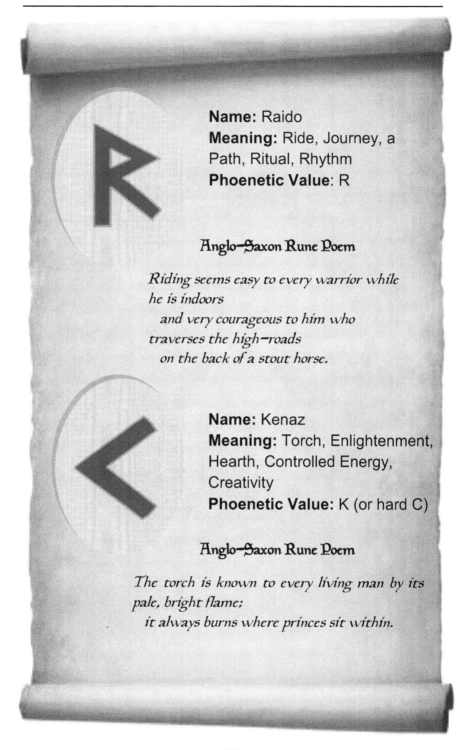

Name: Raido
Meaning: Ride, Journey, a Path, Ritual, Rhythm
Phoenetic Value: R

Anglo–Saxon Rune Poem

Riding seems easy to every warrior while he is indoors
and very courageous to him who traverses the high–roads
on the back of a stout horse.

Name: Kenaz
Meaning: Torch, Enlightenment, Hearth, Controlled Energy, Creativity
Phoenetic Value: K (or hard C)

Anglo–Saxon Rune Poem

The torch is known to every living man by its pale, bright flame;
it always burns where princes sit within.

Name: Gebo
Meaning: Gift, sacrifice, hospitality
Phoenetic Value: G

Anglo–Saxon Rune Poem

Generosity brings credit and honour, which support one's dignity;
  it furnishes help and subsistence
    to all broken men who are devoid of aught
else.

Name: Wunjo
Meaning: Joy, hope, Well Being, Binding, Fellowship
Phoenetic Value: W or V

Anglo–Saxon Rune Poem

Bliss he enjoys who knows not suffering, sorrow nor anxiety,
  and has prosperity and happiness and a good enough house.

Name: Hagalaz
Meaning: Hail, Transformation, Evolution, Destruction, Seed of Primal Life
Phoenetic Value: H

Anglo–Saxon Rune Poem

hail is the whitest of grain;
it is whirled from the vault of heaven
and is tossed about by gusts of wind
and then it melts into water.

Name: Nauthiz
Meaning: Need, Deliverance from Distress, Resistance
Phoenetic Value: N

Anglo–Saxon Rune Poem

Trouble is oppressive to the heart;
yet often it proves a source of help and salvation
to the children of men, to everyone who heeds
it betimes.

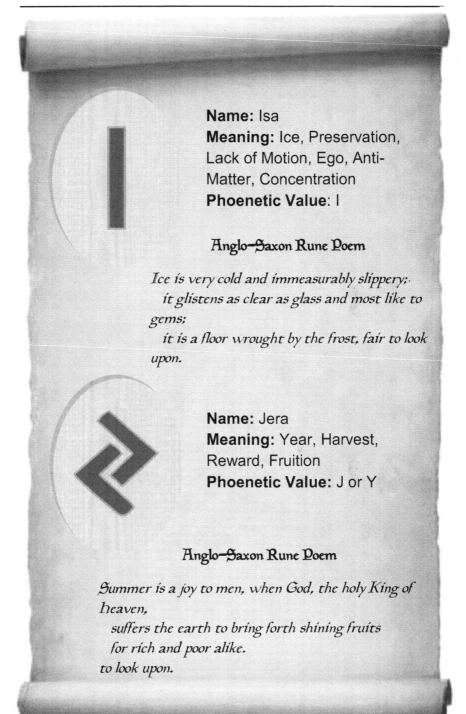

Name: Isa
Meaning: Ice, Preservation, Lack of Motion, Ego, Anti-Matter, Concentration
Phoenetic Value: I

Anglo–Saxon Rune Poem

Ice is very cold and immeasurably slippery;
it glistens as clear as glass and most like to
gems;
*   it is a floor wrought by the frost, fair to look*
upon.

Name: Jera
Meaning: Year, Harvest, Reward, Fruition
Phoenetic Value: J or Y

Anglo–Saxon Rune Poem

Summer is a joy to men, when God, the holy King of
heaven,
*   suffers the earth to bring forth shining fruits*
*   for rich and poor alike.*
to look upon.

Name: Eiwhaz
Meaning: Yew, World Tree, Vertical Cosmic Axis, Life / Death, Protection, Endurance
Phoenetic Value: E

Anglo–Saxon Rune Poem

The yew is a tree with rough bark,
*   hard and fast in the earth, supported*
by its roots,
*   a guardian of flame and a joy upon an*
estate.

Name: Pertho
Meaning: Dice Cup, Chance, Birth, Wyrd, Orlog, The Norns, Time
Phoenetic Value: P

Anglo–Saxon Rune Poem

Pertho is a source of recreation and amusement
to the great,
*   where warriors sit blithely together in the*
banqueting–hall.to look upon.

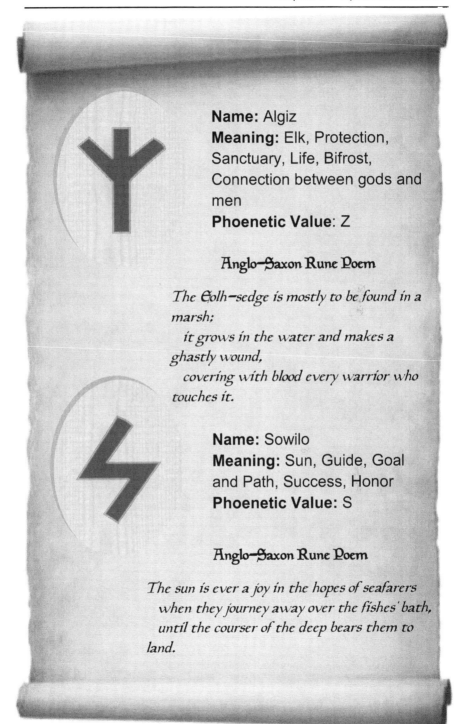

Name: Algiz
Meaning: Elk, Protection, Sanctuary, Life, Bifrost, Connection between gods and men
Phoenetic Value: Z

Anglo–Saxon Rune Poem

The Eolh-sedge is mostly to be found in a marsh;
*   it grows in the water and makes a ghastly wound,*
*   covering with blood every warrior who touches it.*

Name: Sowilo
Meaning: Sun, Guide, Goal and Path, Success, Honor
Phoenetic Value: S

Anglo–Saxon Rune Poem

The sun is ever a joy in the hopes of seafarers
*   when they journey away over the fishes' bath,*
*   until the courser of the deep bears them to land.*

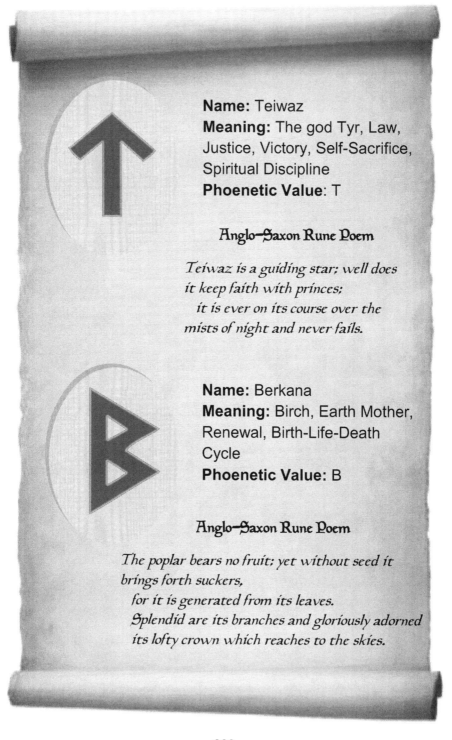

Name: Teiwaz
Meaning: The god Tyr, Law, Justice, Victory, Self-Sacrifice, Spiritual Discipline
Phoenetic Value: T

Anglo–Saxon Rune Poem

*Teiwaz is a guiding star; well does
it keep faith with princes;
   it is ever on its course over the
mists of night and never fails.*

Name: Berkana
Meaning: Birch, Earth Mother, Renewal, Birth-Life-Death Cycle
Phoenetic Value: B

Anglo–Saxon Rune Poem

*The poplar bears no fruit; yet without seed it
brings forth suckers,
   for it is generated from its leaves.
   Splendid are its branches and gloriously adorned
its lofty crown which reaches to the skies.*

Name: Ehwaz
Meaning: Horse, Fertility, Vehicle for Otherworldly Journeys, Trust, Loyalty, Legal Marriage
Phoenetic Value: E

Anglo–Saxon Rune Poem

The horse is a joy to princes in the presence of warriors.
A steed in the pride of its hoofs,
when rich men on horseback bandy words about it:
and it is ever a source of comfort to the restless.

Name: Mannaz
Meaning: Man, Humanity, Intelligence, Divine Structure, Self-Realization, Fulfillment
Phoenetic Value: M

Anglo–Saxon Rune Poem

The joyous man is dear to his kinsmen;
yet every man is doomed to fail his fellow,
since the Lord by his decree will commit the vile carrion to the earth

Name: Laguz
Meaning: Lake, Water, Life,
Growth, Flow, Basic Energy,
Source of Life
Phoenetic Value: L

Anglo–Saxon Rune Poem

The ocean seems interminable to men,
if they venture on the rolling bark
and the waves of the sea terrify them
and the courser of the deep heed not its bridle.

Name: Inguz
Meaning: The God Ingvi Frey,
Potential Energy, Gestation,
Seed
Phoenetic Value: NG

Anglo–Saxon Rune Poem

Ing was first seen by men among the East–Danes,
till, followed by his chariot,
he departed eastwards over the waves.
So the heardingas named the hero.

Name: Dagaz
Meaning: Day, Light, Polarity,
A Turning Point
Phoenetic Value: D

Anglo–Saxon Rune Poem

Day, the glorious light of the Creator, is
sent by the Lord;
  it is beloved of men, a source of hope and
happiness to rich and poor,
  and of service to all.

Name: Othila
Meaning: Property,
Inheritance, Sacred Enclosure
Phoenetic Value: O

Anglo–Saxon Rune Poem

An estate is very dear to every man,
if he can enjoy there in his house
whatever is right and proper in constant
prosperity.

Fylgia Meditation – Contacting your Spirit Guide

Some describe a fylgja[43] as a supernatural being or creature which accompanies a person in connection to their fate or fortune. Others contend that the fylgia is a part of your overall being, yet is semi–independent.

Fylgjur (plural), usually appear in the form of an animal and commonly appears during sleep, but the sagas relate that they could appear while a person is awake as well, and that seeing one's fylgja is an omen of one's impending death. However, when fylgjur appear in the form of women, they are then supposedly guardian spirits for people or clans.

In his books " His Dark Materials" Philip Pullman draws on this theme, and applies a daemon to each person, which is described as an integral part of the persons soul, but takes the form of an independent, or perhaps interdependent, animal.

My Stáv instructor Graham Butcher introduced me to a meditation technique to contact my Fylgia. He guided us through the meditation, which is an ideal way to try this, but if you are doing this solo, here is a transcript of a similar session you can use for reference.

The text below is a transcript of a recorded guided meditation conducted by Philip Brough. I would suggest you record this, either yourself, or have someone do it for you. Then play it back to guide you in the meditation. I used this technique and it was very effective.

I will also include a pre-recorded .mp3 version on my website.

www.northernlore.com

---

[43] Old Norse, literally "someone that accompanies," plural fylgjur

Fylgia meditation - Philip Brough

"You are in a comfortable familiar room. The room is warm and comfortable. The carpet on the floor is warm and soft to the touch. There is a fire in the middle of the room on a raised hearth. There is a small fire burning on the hearth, you feel the warmth on your face. On the fire there is a small grill and also a stove. You look around the room and return to the hearth. You see on the hearth a jug with a drink. Next to the jug there are vessels. You pick one up and feel the weight of the vessel and the texture against your skin. You fill the vessel from the jug and then look down at the drink. You see the reflection in the surface of the liquid. You bring the vessel up to your lips to drink, still watching the reflections, you see your own eyes in the surface as you begin to drink.

When you have drunk, you replace the vessel by the hearth and look again around the room. As you look around again you notice the details of the room. There are doors on each wall. They are old doors, well used and solid. There are carvings around the edge of the door and a raised panel in the middle of each door. You turn to the North and focus on one of the four doors on that wall. You look at the panel and see the Rune carved on it. You focus on that rune, chanting it over and over in your mind

You continue to look at the door and slowly start walking towards it. As you approach, the door slowly opens. You still focus on the rune and watch it . You stoop as you slowly pass through the door all the time focusing on the rune, chanting the sound of it, over and over in your mind.

When you pass through the door, you see the land before you. You travel through the land seeing all around you. You go deeper and deeper into the world, moving closer to a meeting place deep in the heart of the land. You look around you and see all the colors of the land and you stop and listen for a moment and hear the sounds of the land. You move on again moving deeper into this land, continue your journey, proceed until you find a safe place.

293

Once you're there, stop, take a moment to feel the place, you become aware of a presence, turn around and look."

{…breath and meditate on your Fylgia for 5 minutes…….}

"You now feel that it is time to return. You bid farewell to the creature and beings you have met, and you make your way back through the land to the doorway. You still take in your surroundings, the smells, the sounds, the colors. As you approach the doorway, you stoop again to pass through it. When you are back in the room you turn around to watch it close behind you.

You once again look around the comfortable familiar room, and when you are ready you open your eyes."

Bibliography

A. Craig Gibson, E. (1859). *Transactions of the Historic Society of Lancashire and Cheshire, Volume 11.* Liverpool: Historic Society of Lancashire and Cheshire.

Allaby, M. (2007). *Encylopedia of Weather and Climate.* New York: Infobase Publishing.

Antonsen, E. H. (2002). *Runes and Germanic linguistics.* New York: Mouton de Gruyter.

Arthur, R. G. (2002). *English-Old Norse Dictionary.* Cambridge: In parentheses Publications.

Aswynn, F. (2002). *Northern Mysteries & Magick.* St.Paul: Llewellyn Publications.

Bandle, O., Elmevik, L., & Widmark, G. (2002). *The Nordic languages: An international handbook of the history of the North Germanic Language, Volume 1.* Berlin: deGruyter.

Barney, S. A. (1985). *Word-Hoard - An Introduction to Old English Vocabulary.* New Haven: Yale University Press.

Benoist, A. d. (2004). *On Being Pagan.* Atlanta: ULTRA.

Bonweits, I. (1989). *Real Magic.* York Beach: Samuel Weiser, Inc.

Chisholm, J. A. (1994). *True Hearth - A Practical Guide to Traditional Householding.* Smithville: Runa-Raven Press.

Conway, D. (1995). *Celtic Magic.* St. Paul: Llewellyn Publications.

Coulter, J. H. (2003). *Germanic Heathenry - A Practical Guide.* 1st Books Library.

Cunningham, S. (2006). *Encyclopedia of Magical Herbs.* Woodbury: Llewellyn Publications.

Davidson, H. E. (1990). *Gods and Myths of Northern Europe.* London: Penguin Books.

Davidson, H. E. (1999). *Myths and Symbols in Pagan Europe.* Syracuse: Syracuse University Press.

Delaney, F. (1991). *Legends of the Celts.* New York: Sterling Publishing Co., Inc.

Delaney, F. (1992). *Legends of the Celts.* New York: Sterling Publishing Company, Inc.

Desmond, Y. (2005). *Voluspa: Seidhr as Wyrd Consciousness.* BookSurge.

Dunwich, G. (2003). *Dunwich's Guide to Gemstone Sorcery - Using stones for Spells, Amulets, Rituals, and Divination.* Franklin: New Page Books.

Ewing, T. (2007). *Viking Clothing.* Chalford: Tempus Publishing.

Ewing, T. (2007). *Viking Clothing.* Stroud: Tempus Publishing.

Folkard, R. (1884). *Plant lore, legends and lyrics.* London: Sampson, Low, Marston, Searle and Rivington.

Foster, M. H., & Cummings, A. M. (1922). *Asgard Stories - Tales from Norse Mythology.* Boston: Silver, Burdett and Company.

Foster, S., & Duke, J. A. (2000). *Eastern/Central - Medicinal Plants and Herbs.* New York: Houhgton Mifflin.

Giles, D. J., & Ingram, R. J. (890 (1823, 1847)). *The Anglo-Saxon Chronicle.* www.gutenberg.org.

Guerber, H. A. (1895). *Myths of northern lands.* New York: American Book Company.

Gundarsson, K. (2007). *BookSurge Publishing*. BookSurge Publishing.

Gundarsson, K. (2007). *Elves, Wights, and Trolls - Studies Towards the Practice of Germanic Heathenry: Vol. 1*. Lincoln: iUniverse.

Gundarsson, K. (2006). *Our Troth: History and Lore (Volume 1)*. BookSurge Publishing.

Hardwick, C. (1872). *Traditions, Superstitions and Folk-Lore, (Chiefly Lancashire and The North of England)*. Manchester: Simpkin, Marshall & Co.

Hearn, L., & Erskine, J. (1921). *Books and Habits - from the lectures of Lafcadio Hearn*. New York: Dodd, Mead and Company.

Hutton, R. (2001). *The Pagan Religions of the Ancient British Isles - Their Nature and Legacy*. Malden: Blackwell Publishers Ltd.

Jesch, J. (2001). *Ships and men in the late Viking Age: the vocabulary of runic inscriptions and Skaldic Verse*. Woodbridge: The Boydell Press.

Jones, P., & Pennick, N. (1997). *A History of Pagan Europe*. New York: Routledge.

Joseph Bosworth, D. F. (1898). *An Anglo-Saxon Dictionary*. Oxford: Clarendon Press.

Keynes, S., Godden, M., & Lapidge, M. (2004). *Anglo-Saxon England*. Cambridge: Cambridge University Press.

Kouros, Y. (1990, march). A War is going on between my Body and my Mind. *Ultrarunning* , p. 19.

Kraskova, G. (2005). *Exploring the Northern Tradition - A Guideto the Gods, Lore, Rites and Celebrations From the Norse, German, and Anglo-Saxon Traditions*. Franklin Lakes: The Career Press, Inc.

Kraskova, G., & Kaldera, R. (2009). *Northern Tradition for the Solitary Practitioner - A Book of Prayer. Devotional Practice and the Nine Worlds of Spirit.* Franklin: The Career Press, Inc.

Krasskova, G. (2004). *The Whisperings of Woden.* Brooklyn: BookSurge Publishing.

Larrington, C. (1999). *The Poetic Edda.* New York: Oxford University Press.

Lindow, J. (2001). *Norse Mythology - A guide to the Gods, Heroes, Rituals and Beliefs.* New York: Oxford University Press.

Little, E. L. (2004). *National Audobon Society Field Guide to North American Trees.* New York: Alfred A. Knopf, Inc.

Lloyd, J. (1892). *Elixirs and Flavoring Extracts.* New York: William Wood & Company.

Logan, F. D. (2005). *The Vikings in History.* New York: Routledge.

Looijenga, T. (2003). *Texts & contexts of the oldest Runic inscriptions.* Leiden: Brill Academic Publishers.

Mackenzie, W. (1895). *Gaelic Incantations Charms and Blessings of the Hebrides.* Inverness: The Northern Counties Newspaper and Printing and Publishing Company, Limited.

Name, M. (2002). *The Busy Goddess's Hanbook - Quick Reference Guide for the Goddess on the Go!* Provincetown: Sweeney Publications.

Owen, G. R. (1996). *Rites and Religions of the Anglo-Saxons.* New York: Barnes & Noble Books.

Page, R. (1999). *Runes and runic inscriptions: collected essays on Anglo-Saxon and Viking runes.* Boydell Press.

Paxson, D. L. (2006). *Essential Asatru - Walking the Path of Norse Paganism.* New York: Citadel Press.

Paxson, D. L. (2005). *Taking Up the Runes - A Complete Guide to Using Runes in Spels, Rituals, Divination, and Magic.* San Franciso: Red Wheel/Weiser, LLC.

Pennick, N. (1997). *Leylines (Mysteries of the Ancient World)* . London: Weidenfeld & Nicolson.

Pennick, N. (Boston). *Magical Alphabets: The Secrets and Significance of Ancient Scripts -- Including Runes, Greek, Ogham, Hebrew and Alchemical Alphabets.* 1992: Red Wheel / Weiser.

Pennick, N. (2002). *Practical Magic in the Northern Tradition.* Loughborough: Thoth Publications.

Pennick, N. (1992). *Rune Magic.* London: The Aquarian Press.

Pennick, N. (2001). *Sacred Geometry: Symbolism and Purpose in Religious Structures.* Chieveley: Capall Bann Publishing.

Pennick, N. (1997). *The Sacred World of the Celts.* Toronto: Publishers Group West (PGW).

Pennick, N. (1997). *The Scared World of the Celts - An Illustrated Guide to Celtic Sprituality and Mythology.* Rochester: Inner Traditions International.

Peschel, L. (1999). *A Practical Guide to the Runes.* St. Paul: Llewellyn Publications.

Peterson, L. A. (1977). *Edible Wild Plants - Eastern/Central North America.* New York: Houghton Mifflin.

Petrides, G. A. (1972). *Trees and Shrubs - Northeastern and north-central United States and southeastern and south-central Canada.* New York: Houghton Mifflin.

Pitt, R. J. (1893). *The Tragedy of the Norse Gods.* London: T. Fisher Unwin.

Plowright, S. (2006). *The Rune Primer - A Down-to-Earth Guide to the Runes.* Lulu.

Plowright, S. (2000). *True Helm - A Practical Guide to Northern Warriorship.* Petersham: MacKaos Consulting for Rune-Net Press.

Polington, S. (2002). *The English Warrior - From Earliest Times Till 1066.* Wiltshire: Anglo-Saxon Books.

Pollington, S. (2000). *Leechcraft - Early English Charms, Plant Lore, and Healing.* Norfolk: Anglo-Saxon Books.

Pollington, S. (2006). *Wordcraft - New English to Old English Dictionary and Thesaurus.* Norfolk: Anglo-Saxon Books.

Ranking, B. M. (1878). *Bjorn & Bera - A Norse Legend.* London: Remingston & Co.

Richard Inwards, F. (1898). *Weather Lore - A collection of Proverbs, Sayings & Rules Concerning The Weather.* London: Elliot Stock.

Rossman, D. ". (2005). *The Northern Path - Norse Myths and Legends Retold....and What They Reveal.* Chapel Hill: Seven Paws Press.

Shore, T. W. (1906). *Origin of the Anglo-Saxon Race.* London: Elliot Stock.

Simpson, J. (1987). *Everday Life in the Viking Age.* New York: Dorset Press.

Sorensen, V. (1989). *The Downfall of the Gods.* Lincoln: University of Nebraska Press.

Spurkland, T. (2009). *Norwegian runes and runic inscriptions.* Rochester: Boydell Press.

Svenson, R. (2003). *Pierced by the Light: Viking Gods, Runes and 21st Century Magic.* Coalville: Flying Witch Publications.

Thomas A. Wise, M. (1884). *History of Paganism on Caledonia.* London: Trubner & Co.

Thorpe, B. (1865). *A Grammar of the Anglo-Saxon Tongue, from the Danish of Erasmus Rask.* London: Trubner & Co.

Thorpe, B. (1852). *Northern Mythology, Comprising the Popular Traditions and Superstitions of Scandinavia, Norther Germany, and The Netherlands: Volume I. Northern Mythology.* London: Edward Lumley.

Thorpe, B. (1851). *Northern Mythology, Comprising the Popular Traditions and Superstitions of Scandinavia, Norther Germany, and The Netherlands: Volume II. Scandinavian Popular Traditions and Superstitions.* London: Edward Lumley.

Thorpe, B. (1852). *Northern Mythology, Comprising the Popular Traditions and Superstitions of Scandinavia, Norther Germany, and The Netherlands: Volume III. North German and Netherlandish Popular Traditions and Superstitions.* London: Edward Lumley.

Thorpe, B. (1851). *Northern Mythology, Comprising the Principal Popular Traditions and Superstitions of Scandinavia, North Germany, and the Netherlands. Volume 1.* London: Edward Lumley.

Thorsson, E. (1984). *FUTHARK - A Handbook of Rune Magic.* York Beach: Samuel Weiser Inc.

Thorsson, E. (2005). *Northern Magic - Rune Mysteries and Shamanism.* St. Paul: Llewellyn Publications.

Thorsson, E. (1990). *Rune Might: Secret Pratices of the German Rune Magicians.* St. Paul: Llewellyn Publications.

Thorsson, E. (1990). *Runelore - A Handbook of Esoteric Runology.* York Beach: Samuel Weiser, Inc.

Thorsson, E. (1994). *The Truth About Teutonic Magic.* St. Paul: Llewellyn.

Wodening, S. (2006). *Germanic Magic - A Basic Primer on Galdor, Runes, Spa, and Herbs.* Little Elm: Miercinga Rice.

Wodening, S. (2003). *Hammer of the Gods - Anglo-Saxon Paganism in Modern Times.* Little Elm: Angleseaxisce Ealdright.

Young, J. I. (1954). *the Prose Edda.* Los Angeles: University of California Press.

Index

By the same Author:

Northern Wisdom: The Havamal, Tao of the Vikings

The Orient has long shared its ancient wisdom, and so now do the Northmen.

Northern Wisdom presents ancient Viking parables and knowledge in a delightfully accessible modern format.

Combining Teachings on par with Buddha, Sun-Tzu, Myamoto Musashi, Nicollo Machiavelli & Lao Tzu, The Havamal sheds light on forgotten lore of the dark ages.

In the days of the shield-wall, there yet lived poets, scribes and philosophers.

In Northern Wisdom you will:

- Journey through the Mundane and the Mystical passages of the Havamal
- Discover the famed Hospitality of the Northmen
- Learn Maxims for respectable conduct
- Develop the Leadership traits of Heroes
- Explore tips for safe travel in Dark Ages Europe
- Uncover lessons for the bravest Warriors
- Share in the secrets of Odin's Love Quests
- Tap into the power of Viking Magic

The Runes in 9 minutes

Start using the runes in 9 minutes!

In 9 minutes you will be using the runes for personal development and exploration. Of course you aren't going to master the runes in 9 minutes, but you can start!

We'll even teach you how to create your own set of runes. All you need, in addition to this book, is a sheet of paper and something to write with.

This is a book of runes for beginners, and as such, I designed it to be a concise and inexpensive introduction. If you like what you see and the runes are for you, then you can extend your studies. If the runes aren't your thing, then you haven't invested much time or money. Call it a runic sampler if you will.

In The Runes in 9 minutes you will:

- Make your own set of 24 Elder Futhark Runes
- Learn how to use the runes in 3 essential layouts
- Discover a Never Before Published way to use the runes!
- Interpret their meanings in the context of your life
- Study the symbolism of each ancient symbol
- Explore different types of runes such as the Elder Futhark, Anglo-Saxon Futhorc, and Younger Futhork
- Uncover the history and culture behind the runes

Buy directly from the Author at
https://www.createspace.com/3777299
Save 15% - Use Coupon Code: **E8GSAJTG** When checking out

Northern Plant Lore
A Field Guide to the Ancestral Use of Plants in Northern Europe

Over a thousand years ago our Anglo-Saxon ancestors used willow bark to treat headaches; modern pharmaceutical companies use the same basic ingredient - salicin.

Our folk boiled the bark in holy water and added a few other unnecessary ingredients, but they had a basic treatment that worked a millennia ago! And they called this the Dark Ages? Northern Plant Lore explores the plants and herbs used by our ancestors for medicinal purposes, and compares them to the list of plant and herbs proven effective by modern medical science. Not every plant they used worked, but Northern Plant Lore will show you which ones did, and how you can use them today.

In Northern Plant Lore you will:

- Discover Ancient Viking & Anglo-Saxon Remedies Supported by Modern Science
- Grow your own medicinal herbs and plants
- Create remedies at home with the same basis as modern pharmaceuticals
- Know exactly whats going into your body when you take an herbal remedy
- Cross reference ancient cures to modern science
- Browse ailments cross referenced to plants and treatments

Buy directly from the Author at
https://www.createspace.com/3799295
Save 15% - Use Coupon Code: **E8GSAJTG** When checking out

Made in the USA
San Bernardino, CA
11 November 2012